100 ORCHIDS
for the
AMERICAN GARDENER

SMITH & HAWKEN

100

ORCHIDS

for the

AMERICAN

GARDENER

by ELVIN MCDONALD

photographs by STEVEN MCDONALD

WORKMAN PUBLISHING · NEW YORK

*Thanks to Sally Kovalchick at Workman Publishing for planting
the seed for this book in my head several years ago; to John Meils, editor;
to Mary Wilkinson, copy editor; to Hilary Winkler, research assistant; to all the folks at
Hausermann's Orchids, especially Gene and Lynn; and, with extra love and pride,
to the photographer, my son Steven, and the stylist, my daughter-in-law Petra Adelfang.*

TEXT COPYRIGHT © 1998 BY SMITH & HAWKEN

PHOTOGRAPHY COPYRIGHT © 1998 BY STEVEN MCDONALD

LIBRARY OF CONGRESS CATALOGING-IN-PUBLICATION DATA

MCDONALD, ELVIN

SMITH & HAWKEN 100 ORCHIDS FOR THE AMERICAN GARDENER

BY ELVIN MCDONALD

PHOTOGRAPHS BY STEVEN MCDONALD

P.   CM.

ISBN 0-7611-1071-2

1. ORCHID CULTURE. 2. ORCHIDS.

I. SMITH & HAWKEN. II. TITLE.

SB409.M38 1998

635.9'344—DC21   —DC-21   —DC-21

[635.9'344]   98-11201   CIP

WORKMAN PUBLISHING

708 BROADWAY

NEW YORK, NY 10003-9555

MANUFACTURED IN CHINA

10 9 8 7 6 5 4 3 2 1

CONTENTS

APPENDIXES

Preface

Embracing the Orchid

Each of us comes to orchids when we are ready, or is it the other way around? I first met them in all their phantasmagorical array on a visit to the Missouri Botanical Garden's collection in St. Louis. I was 16 years old and attending an annual meeting of the American Gloxinia and Gesneriad Society. This encounter helped me understand the vast world of tropical and subtropical plants and their potential as house and greenhouse plants.

Beginning in 1972, I lived for twenty years in a high-rise apartment in New York City. Membership in an orchid-of-the-month club supplied me with hope, thrills, and definitely some losses. Mostly I remember the morning I raised the blinds in the living room and discovered that a tremendous cattleya hybrid had come back into bloom from new growths brought to maturity in the confines of my apartment.

A deeper involvement with orchids began in 1985, when I worked for a season as a gardener at the Brooklyn Botanic Garden. Some of my most memorable days there were spent helping care for the Garden's extensive collection of species orchids, maintained through the endowment of Danny and Sylvia Fine Kay. On one occasion, Danny himself came to inspect the collection and was completely engrossed as I divided and repotted a morning's worth of oncidiums.

By the time I moved to Houston in 1992, I had a burning desire to have a greenhouse filled with orchids. It was a dream fulfilled more quickly than I could have imagined: the foundation for what had been the previous owner's dog yard measured 8 × 14 feet. All I needed was a small pile of lumber, plastic sheeting for the sides, and corrugated fiberglass panels for the top. Soon, I was in business, or rather paradise, with flowering orchids displayed around a found wood sculpture—a birthday gift from poet Michael Berryhill—and all the others neatly spaced out on benches.

I left all that in the fall of 1995 to join the editorial team at *Traditional Home* magazine in Des Moines, Iowa. At first, I lived in an apartment, a time of challenges and adjustments that was made bearable in part by an array of flowering orchids brought there from Hausermann's Orchids in the western suburbs of Chicago. Beginning last summer, when I moved to a house, my orchid collection has grown exponentially, aided by the increasing availability of an array of orchids in bud and bloom. These can be found at such places as discount chains, home improvement and building supply centers, the supermarket, and, yes, garden centers and nurseries.

Here's to orchids every day for every person who revels in their unique beauties.

—Elvin McDonald
April 1998

A SHORT HISTORY
of a
HUGE FAMILY

O rchids are among the most adaptable and widely dispersed plant families on the planet—found, literally, from the North Pole to the South Pole. Depending on who does the count, there are 800 to 1,400 different genera of orchids, between 17,500 and 35,000 species, and untold hybrids. Orchids began to make their mark on the western world around 1850. Their arrival coincided with the age of the Wardian Case (a wood-and-glass enclosure akin to a small, portable greenhouse), which made it possible to transport them by ship from faraway tropical and subtropical lands. Because of the tremendous effort to acquire them, and their need for heated glasshouses in winter, orchids were initially the sole province of the wealthy.

The early association of orchids with the Wardian Case and its modern counterpart, the terrarium or bottle garden, may be responsible for the widespread misconception that these plants need a close, steamy environment. Although there are exceptions, most orchids thrive in moisture-laden fresh air that is in perpetual motion.

By the end of the nineteenth century, increasing availability of window glass, improved heating methods, and a burgeoning upper

T*he small yellow lady's-slipper,* Cypripedium calceolus *var.* parviflorum, *has fragrant, pouched flowers in spring and grows in northeastern woodlands.*

middle class began to make the pursuit of orchid growing more popular. The American Orchid Society was formed April 7, 1921, inside the treasurer's room of the Massachusetts Horticultural Society in Boston. It was not until after both world wars, however, that orchids began to be acquired and grown by larger numbers of gardeners oblivious to class distinctions.

THE ORCHID ARRIVES

In the early years of indoor growing, the dissemination of orchids moved at a snail's pace because division was the only reliable way they could be propagated. Multiplication was a slow process at best, and tended to preserve any given orchid's rarity and high price. This changed dramatically in 1922 when Dr. Lewis C. Knudson, a professor at Cornell University,

published research showing how to grow orchids from seed.

Knudson stated that viable seeds of almost any orchid could be germinated in large numbers by simply placing them in a sterile, agar-based medium along with nutrients in a glass flask. The practice was dubbed "flasking." When the seedlings were large enough to handle, they were transplanted a half-inch apart into community pots of appropriately fine-textured growing medium. Flasking allowed desirable plants to be available by the armload, not the handful.

The next significant development in orchid propagation came from Yoneo Sagaway at the University of Hawaii in 1959. He showed that it was possible to establish an "ovule culture" or "green-pod" method for seed germination. This process overcame the shortcoming in some crosses where mature seeds fail to develop or inexplicably don't even germinate. Most orchid seeds are now germinated by way of ovule culture.

The first known orchid propagation by the asexual method of tissue culturing—where a new orchid is grown from a piece of a mature plant—was achieved on a *Phaius* grown by John Watkins in the 1940s. It was followed by Gavino Rotor's success with a *Phalaenopsis* from a flower stem. Subsequently, Drs. Georges Morel and Donald Wimber discovered that a 2-millimeter (less than ¹⁄₁₂-inch) cube of meristematic tissue from the growing tip of an orchid stem could be cultivated to grow up to a million mirror-image copies, or clones, of the donor plant. This groundbreaking discovery spurred commercial growers to immediately mericlone superior, award-winning plants.

Almost overnight, a clone coveted at $500 might be readily available at $50 or even $10. Far from depressing the orchid business, cloning has fed an unprecedented demand, not to mention helping the American Orchid Society become the largest such organization in the world devoted to a single plant family. This development, referred to as "tissue culturing," "meristemming," or "mericloning," is considered the single most important discovery in the study of orchids in the twentieth century.

A WORLD OF ORCHIDS

While there may be 35,000 or more orchid species and countless hybrids, most people know a mere handful by sight—cattleyas, phalaenopsis, dendrobiums, oncidiums, cymbidiums, paphiopedilums, and vandas. If these were the only orchids suited to growing and showing at home, they would provide orchid lovers with riches sufficient for a long life of happiness. Since these seven genera represent a small fraction of the

*B*eginning in 1922, the flasking of orchid seeds—sprouting them in a sterile, agar-based medium with vital nutrients added—forever changed the world of orchids.

possibilities, one can easily feel daunted at the prospect of so much complexity, yet each time we learn to grow and flower one orchid, we have opened up the prospect of succeeding with untold others requiring similar care.

CATTLEYA. This popular orchid is found in mainland tropical America. There are 45 to 50 species and innumerable hybrids of *Cattleya*. They are epiphytic, sympodial (having airborne roots and a preference for growing horizon-tally, see p. 8) plants that send up cylindrical pseudobulbs topped by thick leaves from a creeping rhizome. Cut cattleyas have been the premier flower of floristry for a hundred years. The pure white ones are heavenly and the purplish lavender ones define the color "orchid," though they come in many other hues, including orange and scarlet. A large, ruffled lip on the flower, often in contrasting color, is a hallmark of cattleyas. Cattleya flowers are typically fragrant and bloom annually in

Hybrid cymbidium orchids come in a variety of blended or pastel colors, including green. The grassy foliage makes them attractive for display.

almost any season for a period of one to two months; individual flowers last four to six weeks on the plant and about a week if cut. They are borne on a short inflorescence, immediately above the most recently matured growths.

C. *labiata* was discovered in Brazil and brought into cultivation in 1818.

PHALAENOPSIS. Found naturally in India, southeastern Asia, Indonesia, the Philippines, and northern Australia, there are 44 to 46 species and countless hybrids of *Phalaenopsis.* They are epiphytic, monopodial (possessing a vertical growth habit, see p. 8) plants with low-growing, fleshy, long rounded leaves rising from the central crown. Those varieties with white flowers are oftened likened to moths in flight, hence the nickname moth orchid. They come in many colors and may bloom on a short inflorescence close to the leaves or on a long, arching spray, to 3 feet or more. Some are fragrant. Phalaenopsis is one of the best houseplant orchids, and a small collection of only six well-chosen plants can yield blooms every day of the year.

P. *amabilis* was found originally on the Indonesian island of Amboina and first described in 1750.

DENDROBIUM. This huge genus of about 900 species often consternates botanists, but is a delight to the amateur grower. The evergreen types, such as D. *phalaenopsis,* have magnificent tall, canelike pseudobulbs and sprays of long-lasting, showy flowers in many colors. The blooms arise from the tops of new

*A*fter successful pollination, the orchid seedpod develops. When ripe, after several months, it may contain millions of viable though minuscule seeds.

growths matured in the preceding season. These are available in bud or bloom at reasonable prices year-round. Fragrance is common to the primarily winter- and spring-flowering Yamamoto D. *nobile* hybrids. Dendrobiums may be epiphytic, lithophytic (roots that attach to rocks), or terrestrial (earth-bound roots); they are sympodial and may be evergreen or deciduous. They are widely dispersed in India, China, southeastern Asia, Japan, Malaya, the Philippines, New Guinea, Australia, and New Zealand.

D. *moniliforme* (also known as D. *monile,* D. *japonicum,* and D. *catenatum*), from Japan, Korea, and Taiwan, was first described by Carl von Linné in 1753.

ONCIDIUM. Some 420 species of *Oncidium* occur in tropical and subtropical America. They may be epiphytic, lithophytic, or terrestrial, with a sympodial habit and pseudobulbs. Oncidium plant size varies from miniature to several feet tall. Flowering is possible in all seasons, with the often-branching spikes arising from the base of the previous growing season's ripened new pseudobulbs, and lasting four to six weeks. Some oncidium orchids are deliciously sweet-scented. The typical yellow flower assumes the fanciful form of a "dancing lady," which inspires a frequently used common name for the genus.

O. altissimum, from a collection made in the Lesser Antilles (Martinique and St. Vincent), was first described in 1760.

CYMBIDIUM. There are about 50 species of *Cymbidium* from India, southeastern Asia, China, Japan, Indonesia, and Australia. They are variously epiphytic, lithophytic, or terrestrial, with a sympodial habit and pseudobulbs from which sprout grassy, evergreen leaves. Cut flowers of the large-flowered hybrids are second only to those of the cattleya orchid for their popularity in commercial floristry. Miniatures such as Showgirl grow about 2 feet tall, and after several years will form a grasslike clump of leaves to 2 feet in diameter. Above the foliage, upward of a dozen spikes of many flowers grow, and will last for up to two months. Flowering is often in the winter or spring; there are, however, cymbidiums that bloom in summer and fall. Some cymbidiums are even fragrant in bloom. Bloom spikes rise from the base of new pseudobulbs matured in the previous growing season.

C. aloifolium (native to India, Sri Lanka, Burma, southern China, Java, and Sumatra) was first described by Carl von Linné in 1753.

PAPHIOPEDILUM. These are mostly terrestrial, sympodial orchids representing about 65 species from India, Burma, southeastern Asia, southwestern China, Indonesia, New Guinea, the Solomon Islands, and the Philippines. Flowers arise from the center of recently matured growths and may stand barely clear of the foliage or grow 12 to 18 inches above. Hardly any bloom in the kingdom of flora can match the regal, aristocratic bearing of the most lavishly colored and intricately formed paphiopedilums. Collectors of the genus have no trouble managing bloom—from one plant or another—year-round. A slipper- or pouch-shaped lip inspires the common name lady's-slipper orchid; many admirers also refer to them as "paphs."

P. insigne was discovered in northeastern India and sent to England in 1819 or 1820. The lady's-slipper orchids do not respond to tissue culturing.

VANDA. About 40 species of *Vanda* are widespread in tropical Asia, from India to southeastern Asia, Australia, New Guinea, the Philippines, and Taiwan. These epiphytic or lithophytic plants may be small or large, to 6 feet tall or more, with monopodial stems. Flowering spikes grow from the base of the most recently matured leaves and last for upward of two months.

Vandas are known for their blue flowers; some species have figured in producing the most famously blue flowers in the world. The genus dates from 1795.

WHAT ARE ORCHIDS?

J udging by their appearance, it's no surprise that it is the flowers that differentiate orchids from other plant families. The important difference is not obvious at first glance, however, but rather discerned on close inspection, possibly with the aid of a magnifying glass. The epiphytes are unique in particular, with swollen, fat pseudobulbs to store moisture, or obvious air roots that reach out into the atmosphere to collect moisture and nutrients.

Within the orchid family, plants vary to such an extent that any serious attempt at classifying the unknown always starts with an analysis of the flowers. There is even an orchid that has no leaves, only roots. And the first tropical genus ever to reach Europe was the only true orchid that is a vine, *Vanilla planifolia,* brought back from Latin American colonies by the Spaniards in 1510.

TERRESTRIALS AND EPIPHYTES

Orchids are mainly **epiphytes** (living off the air) or **terrestrials** (living off the earth). There are also **lithophytes,** which attach themselves by the roots to rock surfaces and receive the majority of their sustenance from the atmos-

phere and the rain that continually washes over them.

An epiphyte is not the same as a parasite. Parasitic plants are relatively few—mistletoe being one example of a plant whose roots literally plug into the host's vascular system. Being epiphytic *does* mean the need for moist, moving air and a growing medium that sustains moisture and good aeration for the roots. In nature, it also means appropriating a place to live in the superstructure of another plant.

MONOPODIALS *vs.* SYMPODIALS

It is important to recognize at the outset when growing orchids that the kinds grown in pots and by collectors are of two basic growth habits.

*T*his Dendrobium phalaenopsis, *with a sympodial growth habit, shows the rich, velvety coloring typical of this orchid.*

Monopodial orchids, such as vandas and phalaenopsis, grow only one main stem that rises from the growing medium. Flowering stalks appear from the base of the most recently matured leaves. In nature, a monopodial orchid will likely clasp a tree trunk by means of air roots and literally grow away from its origins, constantly seeking light and better position. The lower portions may even die off as new roots above it kick into action, thereby eliminating the possibility of new plants sprouting up from the original roots at the bottom. However, if a vanda has its top removed or has its progress stymied in some way, it's not unusual for one or more new plants to appear along the main stem. When these develop a nice root system in the air, and the leaves are numerous and several inches long, the new plants can be severed from the parent and potted separately. Since monopodial orchids are without pseudobulbs to store moisture, they usually hail from climates that have a fairly uniform amount of moisture year-round.

Sympodial orchids, such as cattleyas, grow horizontally, moving across the surface of the growing medium. They may or may not have pseudobulbs; paphiopedilums, for example, are sympodial in habit but have no pseudobulbs. Sympodial orchid plants can sometimes be divided at repotting time, preferably when the lead new growth approaches the edge of the pot or is actually growing over and beyond it. Flowering stalks appear from the tops of the previous season's matured new growths (as in cattleyas) or from the base of the previous season's matured new pseudobulbs (as in most oncidiums and cymbidiums).

Recognizing an orchid's habit as monopodial or sympodial can help determine its suitability for your growing situation.

ANATOMY OF ORCHIDS

The function of the orchid plant is to reproduce. The fact that its flowers give us great pleasure along the way is of no consequence to the orchid. So clever is the orchid plant that it produces flowers resembling the pollinator it needs to attract. In addition, it gives off a scent telling would-be surrogates that they've found their sexual mate, ready and waiting. It's not unreasonable to suspect that we, too, have been drawn into its web—after all, the better care we give the orchid plant in hopes that it will produce extraordinary flowers, the more likely it will be able to achieve its goal of reproduction.

Orchid roots anchor the plant to a growing place and also absorb

THE NAMES OF ORCHIDS

The rules for naming most plants apply to orchids, but only to a point. Thereafter, additional naming policies have evolved to suit the subject. Understanding orchid nomenclature is a way to make order of a chaotic universe of plants, and to become familiar with terms associated with beauty, performance, or appropriateness of growing conditions.

In catalogs and on name tags, an orchid's genus name appears first, capitalized and italicized (as in *Cattleya*). Outside a scientific context, however, "cattleya" may appear with a lowercase initial letter without being italicized. The second orchid name, generally the species, helps "specify" the plant, and is lowercase and italicized (*dowiana*, as in *Cattleya dowiana*).

A third name indicates a variety or cultivar, for example, *aurea*, in *Cattleya dowiana* var. *aurea*. Hybrid or grex names belong here as well—capitalized, and without italics or single quotation marks. Lastly, there may appear a final, very specific cultivar name, which is capitalized in single quotes, as in 'Rebecca.'

Orchids created by crossing two or more genera are indicated by the placement of a small multiplication sign, or "×," before the reduced abbreviations, such as × Blc. or × BLC for Brassavola × Cattleya × Laelia, or × Slc. or × SLC for Cattleya × Laelia × Sophronitis. Finally, a large "×" preceeding the name of an orchid—for example, × Laeleocattleya—indicates that the plant is a hybrid (in this case between a cattleya and a laelia orchid).

Despite the confusing nature of orchid names, once you buy and grow a few plants, the naming system becomes more familiar and logical. It's also the best way to ascertain an orchid's potential needs, and whether you can provide them—based on their parentage.

*S*mall epiphytic orchids grow along the tree trunks in the tropical rain forest, such as this one in western Java. Along with them grow lichens and mosses, as well as other plants such as gesneriads, begonias, ferns, and aroids.

moisture and nutrients. This occurs whether they are burrowed into a growing medium, extended out into the air, attached to a rock, or something in between. The roots that are exposed to the air will have a green tip and be covered with velamen—a white, spongy coating that absorbs water, shields vital inner tissues, and supports the plant by clinging to surfaces.

One thing specific to orchid plants is the type of growth habit appropriate to their kind; they do not change habits back and forth or become part one and part the other. The sympodial (loosely translated means "feet together") habit features a rhizome that makes new seasonal growths, and proliferates to the point that it can be divided. The monopodial ("one-footed") habit exhibits only one main stem that can grow taller or longer indefinitely, but never sprouts a second stem from the ground. If the sympodial orchid has thickened stems (for the purpose of storing moisture to get it through dry seasons), these are called pseudobulbs.

Orchid leaves may be deciduous or evergreen, thick or thin. Besides healthy roots, nothing is so important to the plant in its goal to reproduce as growing conditions conducive to strong, vital leaves that are able to develop fully and mature through their normal cycle.

Occasionally, a remark is heard to the effect *"Orchid flowers are so beautiful, it's a shame about the plants,"* implying they are ugly ducklings. The true orchid lover embraces all parts of the organism with the same passion—awkward stages and all.

ORCHID FLOWERS.

The primary difference between orchids and other plants is the column, a tiny, fleshy extension from the central interior of the flower that combines both male (stamens) and female (pistils) reproductive organs. In other plants, the male and female parts appear separately within one flower (as in the lily), each on a different type flower on the same plant (as in begonia), or on different type flowers on separate plants (as in holly).

Every orchid flower contains three sepals and petals. The sepals are first seen as the outer sheath for the bud, and later at the 12 o'clock, 4 or 5 o'clock, and 7 or 8 o'clock positions. Two of the petals typically appear at the positions of 3 o'clock and 9 o'clock. The third, at 6 o'clock, will be greatly enlarged as the labellum, or "lip," and may even appear in a contrasting color, with lines in yet another color designed like runway lights to guide the flying pollinator to its destination. Of course, there are exceptions. In paphiopedilum flowers, for example, two petals are modified into one, fused, and enlarged into a pouch. In masdevallia orchids, all three petals are fused into one.

The orchid flower appears asymmetrical, owing to the often unusually large labellum in comparison to the petals and sepals (together referred to as "tepals"). However, if a line is drawn straight down the middle of the flower from top to bottom, it is obvious that the flower is perfectly symmetrical.

REPRODUCTION.

Like many other plants, orchids reproduce by way of pollination. And, they are extremely well adapted to the task. The pollen sits at the front of the column, in the form of waxy yellow balls encased by a membrane equipped with a sticky patch. When an insect or other pollinator crosses this threshold, pollen is deposited in a sticky indentation designed within the recesses of the orchid blossom to receive it. Usually there is also an ingeniously placed membrane that keeps the pollinator from self-pollinating the orchid. The pollinator is, in effect,

A community pot of phalaenopsis seedlings shows—already in its first flowering—the conformation that gives these plants the popular name "moth orchid."

Epiphytic orchids literally take to the air in the warm, moist tropics, or in a simulation of such a climate in a greenhouse or conservatory. They gain sustenance from decomposing leaf mold, nitrogen from the atmosphere, and animal droppings.

flying from blossom to blossom, seeking a meal and at the same time mixing the pollen so as to enrich the DNA of the orchids' seeds. Some orchids are, indeed, self-pollinating, thus illustrating that hardly anything in the complex world of orchids is without exception.

Judging by the way orchids have become highly evolved to work with specific pollinators, it would seem that they are preoc- cupied with propagation. Each species is said to have its own ant, bee, bird, or moth that is unique- ly suited to unwittingly participate in its successful pollination.

The orchid seedpod typically contains a prodigious number of dust-sized seeds. In the first stage of germination, a seed balloons into a green ball called a proto- corm. After a time, roots appear, grow down, and tiny true leaves emerge and grow up.

WHAT ORCHIDS NEED *and* HOW *to* PROVIDE IT

Orchids grow naturally all over the world, from swamp to desert, from tropics to tundra. The famously beautiful lady's-slipper cypripediums, for example, grow wild in Minnesota, where winter can mean prolonged periods of temperatures reaching −50F° and below; other orchids grow near the Arctic Circle. Taming wild orchids and bringing them into successful garden cultivation is one of the standing challenges to all serious horticulturists. And the vegetative increase of the plant constitutes yet another challenge—to perpetuate the species and *also* produce the next season's flowering. Orchids inspire these goals because they are simply among the loveliest and most beguiling of all the floral kingdom.

Despite countless myths that orchids are difficult, they are disarmingly easy once a commitment is made to finding an appropriate place to grow each plant. Well-meaning advice-givers usually warn that it's easier to kill an orchid by overwatering than by underwatering. Consequently, many failures are the result of not watering often enough on a regular, consistent program. Those same advisers may also recommend that too little fertilizer is better than too much, which *is* true. However, orchids respond well to regular applications of fertilizer at the rates recommended on the product label, or with every biweekly watering at one-quarter strength.

T*he calypso orchid* (C. bulbosa) *grows along with lake iris next to a decomposing white birch log. Also known as the fairy-slipper orchid, it grows in cool woodlands and bogs in the northeast of North America as well as in parts of California.*

If you're lucky in matching an orchid plant to an appropriate place, it will appear to thrive on benign neglect. But usually, success comes from paying careful attention to the details and making adjustments as needed from season to season.

HUMIDITY

The largest misconception about orchids is that they need high humidity. Although humidity is a central component to the health of orchids cultivated in pots, the moisture needs to be moving around, carried by fresh, circulating air. A few orchids, notably the jewel orchid (*Ludisia discolor*) and the occasional paphiopedilum, will grow vigorously in terrarium or Wardian Case conditions. In fact, the jewel orchid will produce flawless foliage that is satiny copper with prominent pink veins under closed-environment conditions while being, for all practical purposes, carefree.

Since artificially heated air in a greenhouse, home, or office can be extremely dry, it's beneficial to add moisture to the air (particularly in the immediate surroundings, or microclimate) where orchid plants grow. Not all of the methods to accomplish this are unattractive or purely utilitarian.

One or more orchid plants, in their pots, can be placed on the surface of a bed of water-polished stones contained by a ceramic or other waterproof basin. If the water level is maintained to wet the stones—but never kept so high that the pots stand in it—they will add significant moisture to the air around the plant. When too much water is added to the basin, however, the wicking effect draws too much constant moisture around the medium and orchid roots, and fosters rotting.

There is also a benefit to grouping orchids—and compatible plants such as gesneriads, begonias, ferns, bromeliads, and aroids —in a window or fluorescent-light garden. This way, the moisture evaporating from all the growing mediums and pots has a collective and appreciable impact on humidifying the immediate atmosphere.

Misting the leaves, pots, and growing medium surfaces with water will give everything a refreshed appearance but does little to improve the ongoing moisture content around the plants. Since it can also cause unattractive spotting on the flowers themselves, misting is of questionable value. It's also not a sound practice to leave droplets of water standing at the base of leaves or in the heart of the plant at any time.

Cool-vapor humidifiers provide a reliable means of moisturizing the air for a large window area, a room, or even a house or apartment full of orchids. And if they're kept scrupulosly clean, the moist air given off doesn't constitute a health hazard to those who breathe it. A room with moderate to high humidity (40 percent or more) feels warm to human occupants at considerably cooler temperatures than it does when the air is dry. This results in a savings on heating costs and also averts constant drying of the air—and the orchids.

WATERING

As I stated before, when you start to grow orchids and thereafter when you buy new plants, you'll undoubtedly be warned against overwatering. This advice needs to be taken in context. The greenhouse grower may not, for example, realize how different—and how much drier—conditions are for growing orchids in the home.

In a humid greenhouse or outdoors in the tropics, bark-

A cymbidium orchid will stay beautiful for several weeks, provided it has constant moisture at the roots and the surrounding air is pleasantly warm and moist.

mounted orchids are usually drenched with water on sunny, warm days but never when it's cloudy and cool. Bark-mounted orchids in a house or apartment will need to be dunked in a pail of water at least two or three times a week and misted generously on alternate days. If any orchid consistently dries out too much between waterings, it will gradually decline. The smart orchid grower considers the differences between an orchid's natural environment and the home, compensating whenever possible.

Always use water at room temperature or slightly warmer. Apply evenly all over the surface   not in one spot alone—until water drains from the bottom of the pot. Never leave an orchid pot standing in a saucer or other basin of water. When you place a growing pot inside a decorative cachepot, remove the growing pot before watering; then after watering, set it aside to drain a few minutes before returning it to the cachepot.

A good rule of thumb is to water when the surface is dry. This can be determined by sight according to the color, by touch with the fingers, and also by lifting the pot to tell if it feels light (indicating dryness) or heavy (indicating wetness). Sometimes there can be too much drying between waterings. A potting mix consisting primarily of bark—if it has dried excessively

KNOW YOUR WATER

Water quality should be an important consideration for the health of your orchids. If it's drinkable, it's probably suitable for them. Avoid feeding orchids with water from commercial water softeners that alter it by exchanging sodium for the calcium and magnesium salts, which may force the orchid to absorb too much sodium. The result can be damaged root tips (which are the future of the plant) and blackened leaf tips in cattleyas.

Rainwater can be ideal for orchids, provided it's not polluted by acid rain, drained from a galvanized surface, or coated with chromium, tar and tarlike products, or any possible toxic preservative. It's also necessary to protect the rain barrel or other vessel— to be certain that drainage from orchids or other plants does not

seep back into the reservoir, which could be contaminated with unfriendly organisms. This contamination could subsequently be spread by watering otherwise healthy orchid plants with the same water.

Private wells are used in many areas for watering gardens and collections of potted plants. Especially in coastal regions, check the water yearly to be sure that the quality has not declined. This is also a wise practice in dry climates with annual rainfall of less than 40 inches. In any event, it's best to avoid high concentrations of soluble salts: less than 175 parts per million is best; a range of 175 to 525 ppm is considered excellent to good. Your municipal water department can tell you the soluble salt content of the water supplied to your household.

O*rchids are long-lasting cut flowers. Here, the arrangement includes cattleya, phalaenopsis, and miltonia, along with an African violet and moss ground cover.*

or is fresh—may seem to shed all of its water immediately after repotting. In this case, water lightly, set aside for a half-hour or so, then water generously. Thereafter, water normally according to visible root activity and evidence of top growth.

Satisfying the watering needs of the individual orchid plant is an easy matter. Be mindful, however, of problems that arise in a rapidly expanding collection of different sizes and kinds of orchids in clay, plastic, and possibly other types of growing containers mixed together on benches or shelves. Running the hose or watering can over them in a one-size-fits-all gesture is bound to drown some and leave others underwatered.

POTTING MEDIUMS

One of the first things beginning orchid growers notice is that the growing medium is different from other potted plant mediums. Traditionally, the first mistake made with an orchid is transplanting it to a soil-based medium, or packing sphagnum peat moss in the pot without regard to other factors that affect epiphytic orchid growth.

Until the last quarter of the twentieth century, orchids were often cultivated in pots filled with osmunda fiber or tree-fern bark, or (in warm-climate gardens) in a naturally accumulated, airborne pocket of leaf mold and other organic matter. In these environments, they were further nourished by bird and other droppings. Rain sufficed for watering, and the roots reached out into the air for sustenance and also attached themselves to rough tree bark or any other surface proffered.

With the meristemming of orchids and the rapid increase in the number of orchid hobbyists, the need for an appropriate growing medium grew. This has led to the widespread use of chipped bark as the primary ingredient for mediums available prepackaged from both specialist growers and local garden centers and nurseries. These are typically offered in three grades: coarse, medium, and fine. Which one to use on a given orchid will usually be suggested by the habit, size, and apparent vigor of the plant itself. Seedlings and small divisions are likely to get a strong start in a fine mix. A natural miniature or almost any orchid that adapts to or needs more constant moisture at the roots will also benefit from a fine mixture.

Check the labels on the bags of packaged orchid medium to see if they list the types of orchids for which they're most appropriate. Alternate sources of guidance might include other orchid fanciers in the community and professional growers from whom you purchase the plants.

TEMPERATURE

The vast numbers of different orchids presently cultivated by amateurs and professionals alike can be assigned to one or two of three basic temperature categories: cool, intermediate, and warm. This is *not* an exact or self-limiting requirement for any orchid in particular.

COOL-HOUSE ORCHIDS. The large number of orchids from tropical mountainous regions such as Colombia, Ecuador, New Guinea, and Borneo can be cultivated under cool-house conditions. For these plants, maintain a minimum temperature of around 50°–55°F, increasing on bright or sunny days by 10 to 15 degrees; maximum temperature range would be about 50°–80°F. Some genera in this category include *Cymbidium, Dendrobium* (high-altitude and temperate Australian types), *Lycaste, Masdevallia, Miltonia, Odontoglossum, Oncidium, Pleione* (coolness also required in summer), *Pleurothallis,* and *Sophronitis.*

Orchids from the truly cooler regions of the world are not likely to find happiness in any section of the United States where summers mean high temperatures, with or without a moist or dry atmosphere. However, they can sometimes be grown successfully in areas that benefit from the cooler climate that results from the close proximity of a mountain range, the ocean, a higher altitude, or a cooler microclimate—or even with the use of artificial cooling in a greenhouse.

INTERMEDIATE-HOUSE ORCHIDS. Many popular and rare orchids thrive in this temperature range, with preferences and tolerances similar to the conditions found in many homes, all-season porches, and home greenhouses. Maintain a minimum night temperature of 58°–62°F, increasing by 10 to 15 degrees on bright or sunny days; maximum temperature range would be about 55°–85°F. Included are many species of

Brassavola, Cattleya, Coelogyne, Dendrobium, Encyclia, Epidendrum, Laelia, Maxillaria, and *Oncidium;* also included are *Paphiopedilum* species whose parentage descends from the higher altitudes, and often those paphs with plain olive-green leaf surfaces and undersides flushed with burgundy.

WARM-HOUSE ORCHIDS.

These are among some of the most successful houseplant orchids. Commonly grown cymbidiums, particularly the miniatures, regen-erate mostly during hot summer weather outdoors into quite far north. These plants are often left outside until frost is predicted. This gradual chilling down in autumn, together with decreasing day length, initiates the flower bud-ding. (Orchids in this group can be seriously damaged by sudden chill-ing, especially if they're soaking wet at the time of exposure.) Their minimum nighttime temperature is a balmy 65°F, with a rise of 10 to 15 degrees or more on bright or sunny days; maximum tempera-

POTTING MIXES THROUGH THE AGES

Up until the 1940s, epiphytic orchids were grown mostly in osmunda fiber (osmundine). Increasing demand plus the loss of the osmunda plants' habitat to post-World War II urbanization reduced availability and caused prices to increase sharply. In the 1950s, Hawaiians began growing orchids in tree-fern fiber. As questions of renewable resources came increas-ingly to the fore, chopped dried bark of fir trees was discovered as an excellent medium in the 1960s. As an unused by-product of the lumber business, its widespread use for growing orchids was a palatable solution to everyone.

In 1973, however, tree fern was added to the list of endangered species, and the lumber mills had started burning fir bark as fuel for the drying kilns. As a conseqence, there is no such thing as cheap fir or any other suitable coniferous bark for growing orchids.

Orchid growers have always enjoyed trying alternative growing mediums. If you visit collectors in different parts of the country—whose growing conditions often vary widely—you should observe and ask about a variety of ingredi-ents that are locally adapted, and suited to growing orchids. These may include peat, perlite, bark, charcoal, and plastic foam particles. Other possibilities include crushed lava rock, shredded rock wool, florist foam chips, and materials sold under names such as holite and solite.

Less has changed historically in the growing mediums used for terrestrial orchids. Cymbidiums were originally cultivated in chopped sod, which is also suited to potted amaryllids like clivia, agapanthus, and crinum. Beginning around 1930, coarse sphagnum peat moss came into favor for about twenty years. Then came an explo-sion of new gardeners in the wake of World War II, many of whom had been exposed firsthand to orchids while they were fighting the war. Subsequent experiments included other growing ingredients, such as redwood fiber, fir bark, coarse sand, and charcoal chips.

P*hragmipedium 'Dick Clements'*
will stay blooming for several weeks
in bright light and pleasantly warm
temperatures.

ture range would be about 60°–90°F.

Tropical lowland orchids belong in this category, including the much-loved *Phalaenopsis,* numerous *Paphiopedilum* species (in particular those having silver-mottled foliage), cane-type *Dendrobium, Cymbidium* species with leathery leaves, and *Vanda.* The cymbidiums get along well on the exact regimen given the holiday cacti such as *Schlumbergera, Zygocactus,* and *Rhipsalidopsis,* themselves native to Central and South American rain forests.

LIGHT

Practically everyone who loves orchid growing and strives to share the how-to with others knows it's an inexact science. Fortunately, when it comes to preferable temperatures, popular orchids are tolerant of less-than-ideal conditions,

at least for a season or two. Most orchids tend to be less forgiving in their light needs.

The key light categories are high, medium, and low. Perhaps 25 percent of the orchids popularly cultivated belong to the high or low ends of the scale, while the majority of them belong in a medium range.

Light levels of high, medium, and low can be achieved indoors and out, in windows, under electric lights, on staging or shelving outdoors, in greenhouses, and in a variety of other enclosures devised by determined growers. Hanging plants from the branches of deciduous trees is even a possibility for growing orchids in most climates, at least during the season of warm, frost-free weather.

The right amount and duration of light is something that has to be assessed for every orchid plant brought home, even if it is purchased for display while in glorious bloom. Hot sun shining directly on the flowers can prematurely age them, which is one reason orchid growers often take special pleasure in bringing a plant in bloom to a place indoors, where it can be constantly appreciated in kinder, cooler light.

Later, in the active growing season of regeneration, one learns to observe by the color and heft of the leaves if they are vigorous and adequately supplied with light. An intense dark green often signals insufficient light while yellow-green, bleached, or actual burn spots indicate too much. Healthy orchids at the height of the summer growing season tend to be bright green with slight tinges of yellow.

CREATING *an* ORCHID GARDEN

Chances are, if you want to grow orchids, you have an appropriate place where certain types will flourish without undue fussing or preparation. If not, you may be able to rearrange your furniture or increase the size of a window in order to bring in more light. Never underestimate the importance of finding the right location for orchid plants. In most cases, it can mean the difference between a thriving orchid and a listless, struggling plant. In fact, people who live in dark apartments or houses shaded by surrounding evergreen trees have been known to move to brighter quarters after falling in love with orchids.

Since there is such a large variety of orchids, and they're inherently adaptable, it helps to get to know your own territory, then carefully choose the places where you might grow orchids. How much light do you receive? What are the average high and low temperatures? Is the air moist and fresh? What is the size of the space?

The kind and number of orchid plants that you select must also suit your lifestyle and budget. If you're a frequent traveler for business or pleasure, who will care for the orchids in your absence?

Beautiful orchids can be acquired at almost any price, but they do require an ongoing investment in fertilizers, fresh growing mediums, and larger pots. Naturally, if you want to grow orchids, you will find a way to provide for them. After all, they're among the most reliable tranquilizers and mood elevators ever introduced.

BUYING ORCHIDS

Orchid plants are available by mail order and from local suppliers in larger and larger quantities with every passing year. In both cases, it's

*O*rchids such as the cymbidium thrive in a setting with other houseplants, such as poinsettia, solanum, azalea, and citrus.

possible to purchase seedlings or starter plants as well as those in spike (when the plant is budded and about to come into bloom, or already in full flower). Particularly in and around large cities, orchids in bloom are available year-round. Phalaenopsis and dendrobiums are almost ubiquitous in the flowering gift plant business and are also good plants to buy for your first foray with orchids.

An ideal way to build a collection is to enroll in an orchid-of-the-month program. The supplier will inquire at the outset about the growing conditions you can provide. The purpose is to send you only the orchids—in spike and about to bloom—that are likely to do well over the long haul in your care. This is a good policy because if you're satisfied, you're more likely to continue buying and partici-pating in the supplier's merchandising efforts. For you, it also means investing in a new plant (or at most a few) each month, thus assuring a collection that blooms throughout the year. And it prevents you from acquiring, all at once, more plants than you're able to learn about and care for intelligently.

Membership in the American Orchid Society is recommended for the novice because at the very least, it will provide you with a monthly magazine filled with useful information, inspiring ideas, and the advertisements of many suppliers of starter plants as well as blooming-size specimens. It will also give you access to the social world of orchid lovers, possibly through a local or regional chapter whose meetings you can attend regularly.

WINDOWSILLS

Before moving any plant collection—but especially orchids—to a windowsill, make a point of observing how much light it receives on a daily basis and through different seasons. The houseplants you're growing already are usually a good indicator of light levels.

The direction a window faces is only one factor in how much light is available for growing plants. Trees, shrubs, and the walls of other buildings are common blockers of light. Northern light and good reading light are considered low; eastern light or any area receiving about four hours of sun daily is medium; and southern or western light is classified as high.

Other factors that determine how much light enters a window include the size of the window, the amount of overhang from the eaves, and the latitude. Window gardens in northern regions that experience long periods of snow cover in winter can benefit from the glare on sunny days. (Snow reflects a considerable amount of light indoors to the benefit of all houseplants.) Window gardens in regions where air-conditioning is a constant may have to vie for light because there's often a need to block the sun's heating effect with blinds and draperies.

In addition to the amount of light a window receives, consider the average temperatures, what the highs and lows may be in different seasons, and the air quality of the immediate surroundings. And remember, orchids need fresh air that circulates freely, not drafts of cold or hot air. Be prepared to shield plants that are in the direct line of a heating or cooling vent. It's smart to invest in a maximum-minimum thermometer in order to judge accurately the conditions in any given microclimate.

Another significant factor is the moisture content of the air, expressed as a degree of relative humidity. Because of their often succulent nature, many orchids are equipped with moisture-storing pseudobulbs or canelike stems, or thickened leaves that can exist almost indefinitely in dry air. In order to thrive, flower, and regenerate, they usually need moderate to high humidity (a minimum of 40 to 60 percent, with 60 to 80 percent being more desirable). If this level of humidity isn't present the pseudobulbs may begin to shrivel, a sure sign that the microclimate surrounding the plant is too dry.

WINDOW GREENHOUSES

Small, prefabricated greenhouse units are designed to fit over one or two windows. Generally, these devices are best used over a kitchen sink or adjacent to a breakfast or dining nook. They have the effect of extending indoor growing space and can also bring in more light. Because they are small in volume, air temperatures inside can fluctuate widely, if not wildly, in a matter of minutes or hours. In mild climates or during mild seasons, the adept gardener will find pleasure in using a window greenhouse for growing, showing, and even propagating plants.

ELECTRIC-LIGHT GROWING

Growing orchids under ordinary fluorescent lights can be one of the most effective ways to achieve thriving, regularly flowering plants; and growing them under fluorescent or other electric light is a necessity when window or outdoor light is not available. Not only is controllable brightness assured, but so too is its duration. And a light system for your orchids reduces guesswork to a minimum.

To obtain balanced light rays mimicking those of the sun, suspend a commercial fluorescent reflector fixture (or shop light) 6 to 12 inches above the orchids. Outfit each fixture with a 50-50 combination of at least one cool-white and one warm-white 20-, 30-, 40-, or 74-watt tube. Turn on the lights 14 to 16 hours out of every 24, maintain temperatures of 60°–80°F, keep humidity at 60 percent or higher, and operate a small oscillating fan to keep the air moving.

Low-growing phalaenopsis and paphiopedilums will thrive in such a setup—to mention only two of the nearly endless possibilities. (Orchids particularly suited to growing in a fluorescent-light garden are cited in the specific profiles in Part II of this book, starting on page 44.)

FLUORESCENT TUBES. The electric lamps most commonly employed for growing orchids are fluorescents, which come in a variety of wattages. Two 20-watt tubes over a shelf 1 foot wide by 2 feet long provide the bare minimum for orchid growing, but even this wattage is sufficient to bring into bloom already budded miniatures. Two 40-watt tubes can light a growing table or bench up to 2 feet wide by 4 feet long, and provide a place to grow thriving paphiopedilums and phalaenopsis year-round. Mount four or six 40-watt tubes over the same 8 square feet of growing area and you will have adequate light to grow an even wider variety of flowering orchids.

The next step up is to a 74-watt fluorescent tube, 8 feet long. Four of these tubes mounted parallel, 6 to 8 inches apart on a dull white painted board, and suspended 2 feet above a growing bench about 3 feet wide by 8 feet long, will provide ideal light for a large variety of orchids. Group plants requiring relatively high light toward the center of the tubes, those needing medium light a little off center, and those that will thrive in low light at the ends beneath the tubes, and along the edges of the bench.

Generic cool-white and warm-white tubes are the cheapest on the market. More expensive models are special Agricultural Growth Lamps, which come in the fluorescent-tube configuration. These are color balanced to encourage more uniform growth. Find what is pleasing to your eyes as well as best for the health of your orchids.

The average productive growing life for a fluorescent tube is about a year, or until the end becomes blackened. Brightness can be maintained by dusting the tubes regularly. White walls and ceilings in the immediate surroundings will also maximize the overall effect of the lights.

Placement of the growing fixture depends on the space available and your own priorities. Walk-in closets, guest rooms, porches, basements, attics—all kinds of space can be converted to fluorescent-light gardens. These spaces needn't be used exclusively for orchids, either. Bookshelves that span from floor to ceiling along a wall, perhaps at the end of an otherwise dark hallway, can be outfitted with lights and filled with fascinating orchid plants.

When units for growing orchids are described, some readers will envision utilitarian fluorescent-light fixtures or light units on portable carts with rollers; others will imag-ine only the beautiful plants sustained by them. It's a matter of personal aesthetics. Designers and cabinetmakers are full of ways to hide or obscure the working parts that might be deemed unattractive.

FLUORESCENT ALTERNA-TIVES. The same sorts of floodlights and spotlights used to illuminate and give drama to pieces of art and sculpture can be used to similar effect with orchids. Some growers employ special growth lamps available in these configurations (Wonderlight, for example, from the Public Service Lamp Corporation of New York City) for adding supplementary light to plants not receiving adequate daylight. In either case, the primary

*S*tanhopea tigrina, *from eastern Mexico, is an orchid that sends its flowering spikes through the bottom of the pot, making it well suited to hanging in a greenhouse.*

*C*onservatories and home greenhouses can be filled with a variety of orchids suited to a range of microclimates and lighting conditions.

concern is to make sure that the light rays at the level of the plant, most particularly the uppermost flowers, don't feel overly warm or hot. If they do, increase the distance until there is no perception of artificially warmed air around the orchids. (One advantage of fluorescents is that they are a source of cool light.)

High-intensity lights can take the place of direct sunlight and make it feasible to grow all kinds of orchids without the need for a greenhouse, sunny windows, or a warm climate. Numerous other kinds of light fixtures are used by specialist growers to achieve success. These units may have a high-tech appearance but often give off a color and quality of light that is unpleasant except in short doses.

If you don't purchase complete, assembled light units, it's smart to enlist the help of a licensed electrician and ensure that your light garden is safe to operate. Equipment specifically designed to produce the kind of plant growth responses you want without harm from the constant moisture that goes with orchid growing is always a safer bet than homemade alternatives. A recently published handbook from the American Orchid Society is recommended: *Growing Orchids Under Lights,* by Charles Marden Fitch (American Orchid Society, 1997).

GREENHOUSES

Countless people who pick up, admire, purchase, and bring home an orchid in bloom also harbor a dream of one day having a greenhouse filled with this very kind of plant. A greenhouse of any size is a blessing, but greenhouses require careful planning and their size and placement are crucial to their success.

The smaller a greenhouse is, the more difficult it is to stabilize temperatures during any extremes of cold or heat. If north-facing or unduly shaded, the greenhouse may be a delight in summer but a problem to heat in winter due to a lack of sufficient sunlight. If south-facing and lacking the shade of deciduous trees in summer, the greenhouse can be impossible to light, shade, and cool sufficiently to be an asset.

Deciding on a constant temperature for your greenhouse will be a primary concern. If it's small, one range, such as cool in winter, may be all that's feasible. If it's moderate to large (a minimum of 200 to 300 square feet), two ranges may be accommodated—cooler toward the ground, warmer toward the roof. It's wise to invest in a maximum-minimum thermometer at the outset, to remove the element of guesswork in determining where to place different orchids.

A greenhouse that opens off a room of your home can be ideal. In such a situation, it's often possible to engineer the home heating and cooling system to regulate temperatures within the greenhouse. One of life's supreme pleasures is to step directly into your own dark-

PREFABRICATED GREENHOUSES

Prefabricated greenhouses typically embody engineering that helps accommodate glass or plastic fittings, and are designed to keep out water and cold while admitting the maximum amount of light. The best designs allow for the runoff of condensation so that it doesn't drip constantly on the plants or drain and collect, rotting any wood parts. Prefabricated greenhouses are also cheaper per square foot to erect than almost any other form of room construction.

Not all prefabricated greenhouses have a utilitarian look. There are elegant Edwardian glasshouses and numerous other styles that are pleasing to the eye. A custom-built greenhouse may also be the answer, for reasons of practicality (such as having on hand a large number of salvaged sashes) or for placement in a grander setting where an architect-designed structure is indicated.

ened greenhouse on a cold winter's night and have the orchids gradually reveal themselves in the pale moonlight. The purity of white blossoms, nocturnal fragrances, and sculptural forms is a rare treasure indeed.

SLATHOUSES

Often, slathouses are simple and utilitarian constructions of lath or slats of wood nailed parallel on frames and set into a vertical structure to make a "house." The narrow pieces of wood must be installed in a north–south direction at a distance equal to their own width apart. This way, the sunlight moves gradually across the plants instead of lingering too long in one place, which would burn the foliage.

Saran and other shading cloths have put a modern spin on the slathouse. These durable, usually dark green fabrics can be attached to wood or metal frames and obviate the need for slats or laths.

The slathouse can also take the form of a dressy lattice design, especially as a façade for what may otherwise be a working place to grow orchids throughout the warm season. A potting bench and storage units can also be kept in such a structure, along with the stakes, ties, and dress-up pots used for displaying orchids in the house.

It's important that benches in a slathouse be designed to facilitate rapid drainage of excess rain and free air circulation. Half-inch wire hardware cloth on a strong wood frame is excellent for this purpose.

ORCHID GROWING IS SIMPLE

O rchids are no more difficult to grow than begonias, geraniums, or philodendrons. Their needs may be somewhat different, but they can be grown with ease as long as their differences are respected. What separates orchid culture from that of common houseplants, and even other exotics, is the treatment of their unusual roots and growing mediums.

With most plants, the gardener may prune back the roots en masse at potting time or tease them out from a rootbound mass—they're not really dealt with as individuals. With orchids, it's wise to examine each and every root when repotting, and to remove any that are not alive and well.

Because orchid roots are fewer and more sensitive than ordinary plant roots, a standard potting medium will not do; an open, porous medium that allows a free flow of air and moisture is more apt to make for healthy growth. In nature, most orchids live attached to trees or rocks, with their roots exposed in the open air. When cultivated indoors, their home needs to be as similar to their natural environment as possible. Most potting mediums for orchids are made of different combinations of bark, peat moss, sand, and sometimes charcoal and perlite.

When their root and potting medium needs are met, most orchids will thrive. The smart beginner will, however, start with a relatively small number of orchid plants whose cultural requirements correspond with the growing conditions that can be easily provided. Beginning with less demanding orchids will enable you to learn at a comfortable rate without feeling pressured to know too much, too soon.

POTTING AND REPOTTING

The chief difference between repotting an orchid and repotting most other plants is that the orchid's old growing medium must

Clay orchid pots with extra drainage holes or cuts in the sides help ensure that the roots of epiphytic orchids receive adequate air and prevent them from standing in excess water.

be discarded in its entirety. In addition, every root should be carefully examined and any traces of dead tissue removed.

Flowering-size orchid plants usually need repotting every two years. Seedlings and young divisions may need to be repotted after a year, sometimes sooner. Underpotting may stunt growth, but overpotting is far more dangerous and can lead to overwatering and loss of the plant through root rot. A pot that is unnecessarily big also wastes water, fertilizer, and growing space. A poorly chosen pot is often responsible for many of the problems encountered by first-time orchid growers.

POTS. Orchids can be grown successfully in clay or plastic pots with standard drain holes or additional cuts made to facilitate the extra drainage and aeration appreciated by epiphytic orchids. Moisture transpires through the walls of unglazed clay and can serve to help humidify the air immediately surrounding plants. Orchids in unglazed clay, however, will dry out more quickly than those in plastic—or any nonporous material—and thus require more frequent watering. Clay is also a much heavier material than plastic, which certainly should be a consideration when orchids are grown commercially and subsequently shipped over long distances.

Some orchids are grown in wood-slat, wire, or plastic mesh baskets designed to be hung in the air. Vandas and related plants such as ascocendas and rhyncostylis are often seen in this kind of container outdoors in the tropics. The same plants may do better in azalea pots or bulb pans in a temperate region with drier air.

Like most plants, orchids tend to thrive in pots matched to their overall size. Small orchid plants are suited to pots 2½ to 5 inches in diameter; medium plants require pots 6 to 8 inches in diameter; and large orchids pots should be 9 to 12 inches in diameter. Specimen-size cymbidium hybrids are sometimes grown in tubs up to 18 inches in diameter.

A clay pot can be one of three standard heights: regular (as tall as it is wide across the top), azalea or three-quarter (three-fourths as tall as it is wide across the top), and bulb pan (half as tall as it is wide across the top). Long Tom and tall bonsai pots, about one and a half times as tall as they are wide across the top, are ideal for displaying certain orchids in bloom. But Long Toms are too deep for most orchids unless the bottom half is filled with coarse drainage material. Miniature cymbidiums are an exception to

WHEN TO REPOT

It's always best to repot before the growing medium starts to break down or decompose. Particularly if the pot is deep or free drainage is in any way hindered, growing medium toward the bottom may decompose and begin to have an adverse effect on the plant before any evidence becomes visible at the surface. Be conservative in moving to a larger pot: a small orchid plant in a big pot is more likely to succumb to overwatering than a big one in a small pot is likely to die from drought.

Repot sympodials such as cattleya and encyclia right after flowering or as roots can be seen emerging from the new lead. Repotting is in order when growth reaches the pot rim or in any event before it has extended much beyond. The oldest pseudobulbs, by now leafless and called "back bulbs," may be removed as part of repotting. If firm and healthy, they can be used for propagation. Drop them in a clear plastic bag with some moist sphagnum moss and hang the bag in a bright, warm place out of direct sun; remove and pot up when new roots and leaves show.

Repot monopodials such as vanda and phalaenopsis at any time during active growth. If you are growing under fluorescent lights and can maintain ideal temperatures and humidity for active growth, repotting plants at the stage when they need it can be done without regard to the season outdoors. Orchids grown by daylight are mostly repotted in the period between late winter and early summer.

If for no apparent reason an orchid is not doing well, try repotting. In the process you may discover that the growing medium has broken down (is actively decomposing or rotting) and that the plant's roots have started to rot. Carefully prune back to healthy tissue and repot in fresh medium. Water well at the outset, then very cautiously until the roots have reestablished and top growth becomes evident.

HOW TO REPOT

Orchids may be different from other plants grown in pots, but they are typical in their need for regular and timely repotting. Repotting should usually occur immediately or soon after flowering, although not in all cases. Another window of opportunity is at the onset of the active growth season, generally at the end of winter or beginning of spring.

1 *Lots of roots present outside the pot and the relative size of the plant suggest that it's time to transplant.*

2 *Remove the orchid plant from the pot and clean off the old medium. Remove any dead, broken, or rotted roots.*

3 *Position the plant in a larger pot— keeping the plant at the same level as its previous pot—and add fresh growing medium.*

4 *Rap the pot lightly against the bench to help settle the medium. Chopsticks may also be used to work the particles of medium into contact with the orchid roots.*

this potting rule because they can grow well and look artful in a Long Tom or tall bonsai pot, provided it has a large, unblocked drain hole.

Plastic pots may be round or square and usually have the same height/width ratio as a three-quarter clay pot. Eager propagators and those who grow on seedlings in community pots (containing numerous plants) often favor 3- or 4-inch square pots to maximize available space. But this can be an unwise practice unless air circulation is sufficient to keep crowded roots from fostering disease.

HOW TO REPOT. If you treat repotting orchids the same way you do the common houseplant, even under ideal conditions, the results will likely be disastrous. Orchids respond better to repotting that is slow and deliberate, root by root, plant part by plant part. When everything dead has been clipped away, the living roots can be respectfully positioned in a clean pot with fresh growing medium purposefully added in a slow, almost continuous movement. This way, the plant will settle at the desired height and the growing medium can be gently pushed against the roots.

Before unpotting, assemble the materials you will need for repotting: growing medium, clean pot, and sterile pruners or floral scissors for trimming dead roots. The ideal place is a potting bench with a nearby utility sink, garbage can, and separate receptacle for anything you wish to compost. In an apartment, the kitchen counter and sink will work nicely as the basic setting for orchid care and maintenance.

Work with only one orchid plant at a time—to prevent spreading an insect or disease problem unwittingly. Wash your hands before repotting each plant, using soap and warm water, and sterilize cutting tools by leaving the blades submersed in denatured alcohol for 15 to 30 minutes. Rinse them in

IF YOU FIND INSECTS WHILE REPOTTING

One of the beauties of being in such intimate contact with an orchid when repotting is that you can detect the slightest beginnings of an insect infestation. If you have trouble seeing details sharply, use a magnifying glass, work in ideal reading light, and if all else fails, invest in some new eyeglasses. Whether you detect a few insects or an appalling infestation, treating the plant out of the pot and fully exposed is the easiest way.

The problems most often found will be mealybugs and other scale insects, brown bumps, or white or oyster-shell-like bodies. A great part of the population can be gotten rid of by removal with your fingers. Rinse off all the residue with a stream of running water, and set aside to drain. When the plant is dry, go back over it using a magnifying glass and rub off any remaining insects with a cotton swab dipped in denatured alcohol. Thereafter, isolate the plant and repeat the previous treatment on a weekly basis until you can confidently give the plant a clean bill of health and return it to the usual growing area.

*O*rchids sold in bloom, such as these lady's-slippers or paphiopedilums, may have recently been repotted—or not. After flowering is usually a good time to repot.

water and dry them thoroughly before beginning another orchid.

When unpotting an orchid, take great care not to break any new leads (young shoots) or vital roots. New leads are particularly vulnerable; these crisp, tender shoots will snap off at the slightest false move on your part. In no phase of gardening is the phrase "make haste with deliberate slowness" more apt than when repotting an orchid. Sort out the living roots and other growing parts from the dead ones, removing anything not alive.

When repotting a sympodial orchid, position it with the oldest growth against the rim of the pot and the new lead headed toward the opposite side; keep the rhizome essentially level in the pot. If repotting a monopodial orchid, position it so that the main stem emerges from the center of the pot.

Apply room-temperature or slightly warmer water across the growing medium's surface and set the plant aside to drain. If the medium was quite dry, water it again after an hour or so. Following this initial wetting, go easy with water until the plant has taken hold, then gradually increase according to its individual needs, the season, and the environment.

Sympodial orchids usually need some anchor in order to be kept secure and upright in the fresh growing medium until the roots can establish. Various wire pot clamps and clips are sold for just this purpose.

Monopodial orchids that grow tall, such as vandas, may benefit from a bamboo, wire, or picturesque twig stake inserted next to the base of the plant. Supports are best inserted immediately preceding the addition of new growing medium around the roots. Adding the stake after potting or at some later date is possible, but there may be some resistance from bark chips or living roots, which can lead to forcing the stake, or breaking it and possibly damaging the orchid plant.

GROWING MEDIUMS

In nature, epiphytes grow on tree trunks, usually first establishing in the crotch formed by a branch where it emanates from the trunk; lithophytes attach to rocks, with the roots gaining most of their sustenance from the atmosphere. The biggest mistake you can make in potting up such orchids is to think that good garden soil enhanced with a dollop of compost or other humus will meet the normally airborne orchid plant's needs. It won't. Confusion generally arises because the word "compost" is used to mean "growing medium" in many orchid texts. In fact, the compost known to American gardeners is not used in *any* recommended growing medium for orchids.

Following are three basic growing mediums for a range of different orchids. They are specifically recommended by type for every orchid listed in Part II of this book.

GROWING MEDIUM A

*6 parts coniferous bark such
    as pine
1 part perlag (perlite) or pumice
1 part coarse sphagnum peat moss
1 part horticultural charcoal*

Suitable for all epiphytes and some terrestrials, this medium is prepared (and sold by orchid specialists and at most local garden stores) in three grades, to be used according to various pot and plant sizes:

- FINE
    bark particle sizes 1–3 mm
- MEDIUM
    bark particle sizes 4–6 mm
- COARSE
    bark particle sizes 7–12 mm

Extra-coarse mixes may be used for large specimens of genera such as *Angraecum* and *Vanda.* When available and in areas with soft water, chopped green sphagnum moss is good for fine-rooted orchids such as *Masdevallia, Odontoglossum,* and *Pleurothallis.*

WHEN TO RETAIN OLD POTTING MEDIUM

Not all orchids grown in a moist tropical environment need complete repotting at regular intervals. Vandas, asocendas, rynchostylis, dendrobiums, and oncidiums, in pots or wood cradles filled with a non- or slow-decomposing medium such as chunks of tufa or cork, can be set intact into a larger container and additional growing medium added to fill between.

Bark-mounted orchids are sometimes left to establish a colony, which can take several years. Any parts of the plant that may die back can be removed with pruners or floral scissors. When it's time to establish a new mount, provide cushioning for the offset with live sphagnum moss and bind everything with clear nylon fishing line.

A nguloa × Rolfei, *a variety of the cradle orchid, is a terrestrial native to tropical South America and suited to cool greenhouse culture and Growing Medium B.*

Inert substances such as rock wool, which degrade less rapidly than pine or other coniferous bark, have also been used in growing mediums. Plastic foam peanuts and even the corks saved from wine bottles can prove useful for filler in the lower recesses of a pot that might otherwise drain poorly. Wine-bottle corks are even used whole as an extremely coarse medium, or broken up for a more common medium-to-coarse mix.

GROWING MEDIUM B

1 part sphagnum peat moss
1 part loam
1 part clean, sharp sand

This medium is designed for most terrestrial orchids. Terrestrials may be earth-based, but they are more likely to grow in nature where there is an abundance of humus to hold moisture and aerate the roots simultaneously. Coarse sand, small stones, or chips further assure aeration and rapid drainage of excess water. Initially, cymbidiums in cultivation were grown in chopped turf. Today they and other terrestrials are grown variously in almost any medium comprising at least 40 percent organic matter.

Orchid specialists sell bags of growing medium mixed for terrestrials (such a specialized product may not be available at a neighborhood garden shop). A convenient shortcut is to use two to three parts of a packaged soilless, peatlite mix, such as Pro-Mix, in combination with one part of fine-to-medium bark chips.

GROWING MEDIUM C

6 parts fine bark chips
3 parts sphagnum peat moss
3 parts chopped live sphagnum
  moss

This is a finer rendition of Growing Medium A, designed for fine-rooted orchids and seedlings. Some growers favor this type of mix for phalaenopsis and paphiopedilums. It can also give excellent results with the popular miniature cymbidiums.

HARDENING OFF AND DORMANCY

Orchid growth tends to follow the ebb and flow of the seasons outdoors, and is most active from late winter to late summer. The growth gradually winds down through the waning days of autumn until plants reach a state of semi-dormancy. This usually lasts until longer days and increasing temperatures coax them back into activity. (For specific blooming information, see Part II, starting on page 44.)

Evergreen orchids retain their foliage all year. For these plants, semi-dormancy amounts to a small rest precipitated by cooler temperatures, less light, reduced watering, and the withholding of fertilizer. Generally, orchids with pronounced pseudobulbs (as in *Cattleya*) or thickened canes (as in *Dendrobium*) can be kept drier than those with thickened leaves (as in *Phalaenopsis* and *Paphiopedilum*).

Some deciduous species lose their leaves naturally at the end of the season; an example is *Malaxis*

latifolia, which appears to collapse overnight. If you should find this particular orchid or another deciduous species in a yellowed heap, don't be alarmed. Remove the spent leaves, withhold fertilizer, and water only enough to keep the growing medium from being bone-dry until the beginning of the next growing season.

FERTILIZING

Airborne orchids in nature exist on a comparatively lean diet, receiving atmospheric nitrogen during rainstorms and fertilizer from animal droppings. In cultivation, orchids depend on us to provide nutrition. Garden shops and specialist growers sell at least one or more fertilizers labeled specifically for orchids, in liquid or granular form (for dilution in water). Also available are timed-release pellets (14-14-14 is a common favorite), the perfectly balanced, "play-it-safe" formula for a constant feed of nitrogen, phosphorus, and potash (NPK) at usual growing temperatures. Fluorescent-light growers rely on 14-14-14 and, to avoid doubling up or skipping, keep records of application dates. In practice, 14-14-14 timed-release pellets are used almost wherever orchid plants are in a position to have encouraging growing conditions for at least three months following the application, whether indoors or out, under lights or in daylight.

Orchids planted in bark-based growing mediums also need applications of 30-10-10 (the popular brand Miracid was originally formulated for orchids). The extra nitrogen benefits both the plant

F*aithful, consistent watering and fertilizing produce orchids with many long-lasting flowers, such as encyclia, phalaenopsis, and paphiopedilum.*

and the organisms at work decomposing the bark. Fish emulsion and liquid seaweed are also used in this way.

Blossom-booster formulations such as 15-30-15 promote flowering and stem strength. These fertilizers should be applied at the outset of the bud formation season, or to vigorous orchid plants that have not recently flowered. Always mix fertilizer at the strength recommended on the product label. Be consistent, and mark application dates on your garden calendar. Experts agree that increasing or haphazardly "doubling" the rate is almost never a good practice. Also worth questioning is the ubiquitous recommendation that all fertilizers be applied at half-strength.

If an orchid plant is extremely dry, water it first and give it several hours or overnight to rehydrate. Then apply a fertilizer that has been diluted and well mixed in the watering can. Feed uniformly over the entire growing-medium surface, not in one place only. Hanging plants that include bark mounts benefit from dipping or brief submersion in fertilizer solution. When using timed-release pellets, always wear rubber or vinyl gloves, measure the application, and distribute the pellets evenly over the surface, not bunched in one place.

Regularly fertilized orchid plants will also benefit from occasional flushing of the growing medium with plain water. After draining for a half-hour or so, repeat the flushing; this may be done numerous times over the course of a day. An indication of the need for flushing is the buildup of mineral salt encrustations on the pot rim, around the drain holes in plastic pots, and on the exterior of clay pots.

Advanced amateurs and professional growers often practice a fertilize-with-every-watering regimen. This method involves diluting the fertilizer to one-fourth or one-fifth the usual strength and applying it with every watering, except for a once-weekly flushing with plain water. Executing intensive culture like this demands unusual commitment but produces beguiling results.

INSECT AND DISEASE MANAGEMENT

Orchid plants in the peak of vigorous health and bloom can seem invincible, magically protected from anything as unpleasant as devastating attacks of opportunistic insects, diseases, viruses, and vermin. They are not. As with other plants, disease is often related to some particular stress. A virus may infest a plant already under duress from one or more primary stresses, such as poor air quality, a decomposing growing medium, or inadequate light.

The orchid plants distributed in commerce are remarkably healthy and deserving of a clean bill of health. Under the best of circumstances, however, the commercial distribution process is stressful to the plants. Be watchful for any of the maladies described here, and try not to bring any of them home on new acquisitions. If a plant is in any way suspicious, isolate it until you ascertain what is wrong with it. Insects, diseases, and viruses all travel by their own means at the appointed time. Crowded plants are vulnerable by definition.

For humans, cleanliness is put next to godliness. The same applies to orchids. Nothing about their cultivation is as paramount to good health as the maintenance of clean space and prompt removal of dying or dead plant parts.

WEEDS. Keep weeds away from orchids—out of their pots and away from the greenhouse. Purists even advise keeping all other plants at some distance because they might harbor pestilence and thereby constitute a threat to long-term orchid health. One of the most widespread pot weeds of orchids and of greenhouse underbench

Hybrid cymbidium orchids are nearly free of insect and disease problems, provided they are well cared for. Inspect regularly, however, for signs of problems such as brown scale.

*L*ady's-slipper orchids such as this paphiopedilum can bear a dozen or more flowers at once when well grown. They look beautiful displayed with delicate maidenhair fern.

areas is *Oxalis corniculata.* This reddish to green plant seeds prodigiously, grows almost overnight, moves around, and roots deeply. When oxalis in a pot looks healthy, in all likelihood so too will the orchid. But the day you notice the oxalis is looking sickly will likely be your wake-up call that the orchid is severely stressed. Get rid of the oxalis, even if you have to unpot the orchid and evict the oxalis root by root.

Ferns can also seed into orchid pots and will behave as weeds unless removed. Eradicating ferns may require unpotting, crumbling away the growing medium, and delicately sorting out the orchid from the intruder.

Another shameless weed often found in orchid pots is a member of the acanthus family, possibly a *Chamaeranthemum.* It has round-

ed silvery leaves and jumps like a rabbit from sprout to flower to seeding. While these small plants stay close to the orchid growing medium in near rosette fashion, the roots go to astonishing depths in a matter of days. As with oxalis, complete removal and constant vigilance are required to keep this weed out of a collection once it appears.

Weeds in orchid pots have a way of making a collection appear out of sorts. They also use water, nutrients, light, and air—all resources better dedicated to the orchid plant. When cultural stress occurs, opportunistic insects often take over, including a variety of scales, spider mites, and occasional thrips.

INSECTS. Scale insects are common to orchids and can be a serious threat to a single plant, if not an entire collection. These insects drop honeydew on the leaf surfaces, which in turn hosts sooty mold. In fact, the sight of mold is often the first clue that a plant is under siege from one kind of scale or another: armored, soft, pit, or mealybug. Removal by hand, using cotton swabs dipped in denatured alcohol, is possibly the safest way to rid an orchid of unwanted creatures (and the most effective if you use a magnifying glass, work in good reading light, and repeat the treatment every five to seven days). These insects establish in crevices and between layers of plant tissue. Inspect and treat every out-of-the-way place where insects can establish a home.

Damage from thrips is perhaps more widespread than most gardeners realize. The insect itself is tiny, threadlike, and black. Typically, it feeds on floral parts, rasping away the tissue and causing malformed flowers. Thrips are also known carriers of bacterial, fungal, and viral infections. If detected, the plant should be sprayed with a solution of water and insecticidal soap.

Spider mites are tiny and may be variously colored, but are usually reddish. They cluster on the undersides of leaves and will, if unchecked, eventually web the plant and floral parts. The presence of spider mites indicates dry conditions, especially a lack of air moisture and poor air quality. Plants under any stress from lack of light, water, or nutrition are most likely to succumb to spider mites. Treat plants by correcting these conditions and spraying with insecticidal soap and water—especially directing the treatment toward the leaf undersides.

If you have an orchid collection, don't be surprised if the things that go bump in the night turn out to be cockroaches, caterpillars, snails, slugs, or mice eating the very buds you were preparing to worship as glorious new flowers. When it happens, try not to fret; take revenge instead. Set traps. Go on surprise flashlight raids in the dark. Contemplate the joys of delayed gratification.

DISEASES. There are a host of fungal diseases that can trouble orchid plants, especially in the presence of abundant water and high humidity, and in temperature extremes of both hot and cold. When disease occurs, immediately isolate the plant. The disease will usually manifest itself as rotted or discolored tissue in some part of the plant. This can occur at any point from root tip to pseudobulb or leaf to flower-bud tip.

If you discover any form of disease, sanitize the plant and inspect the discolored area. Reduce the amount of water that you give the plant and minimize water left on the leaves. Increasing the air circulation will also benefit the overall health of the plant.

When new growth appears healthy, trim out any remaining damaged parts. If decline and death occur, discard all the remains, including the growing medium. Sterilize the pot by soaking it overnight in household bleach and water mixed at a ratio of 1:9, then rinse well in plain water.

Viruses are the most worrisome threat to cultivated orchids. The first was described in 1943, and since then about twenty different types have been identified. The two most common are cymbidium mosaic virus and tobacco mosaic virus. The effects are overall yellowing (chlorosis), death of tissue, and restricted or stunted growth. There may also be streaking in the floral parts. Ringspot on the leaves is a sign of tobacco mosaic virus. Be aware that almost any of these symptoms can be traced to problems of nutrition, chemical imbalance, excessive salts in the water supply, insects, or damage from sprays.

Be finicky about cleaning and grooming your orchids and the area in which they grow. It's the best defense against virus and most other orchid pestilence.

ORCHID TROUBLESHOOTING

SYMPTOM: Dark green, apparently healthy leaves but no bloom.
CAUSE: Insufficient light. Too much nitrogen. (A flush of soft new growth from the use of too much high-nitrogen fertilizer may quickly host a thriving colony of greenish aphids.)

SYMPTOM: Leaves stay limp, shriveled, or in a dead wilt despite regular watering.
CAUSE: Root rot, due to overwatering or a pot without drainage. Orchids are especially vulnerable if chilled at the same time that they are overwatered. This end effect— root rot—can also begin through habitual underwatering, or permitting plants to be excessively dry in the presence of high light and high temperatures. Depending on the type of orchid and the climatic origins, some are better able than others to revive after extreme, protracted dryness. In many cases the plant that is desiccated to death or near death is suddenly subjected to heavy watering and an extra-strength dose of fertilizer. It may linger in this doomed state for months or even years, but the ultimate blame is on overwatering.

SYMPTOM: Flowers on a purchased plant or on one grown in a greenhouse or under lights wilt, fade, discolor, and drop at a disappointing rate, particularly after being put on display in the house.
CAUSE: Change in environment. Adequate light is needed to sustain the flowers and any buds remaining (of course, no hot, direct sunlight except possibly for brief times early or late in the day). Avoid heaters, coolers, fireplaces, and the TV, and take care that spotlights or floodlights are not placed too close to the flowers.

SYMPTOM: After a deep chill or possibly frost or light freezing, leaves become limp, transparent, or blackened.
CAUSE: Cold shock. Don't be too hasty to cut back or discard. Sufficient old growth may survive to send out new shoots when conditions improve.

A KEY *to the* FIELD GUIDE

P hotographs of all orchids in the Field Guide were taken in the spring, summer, and early fall of 1997 in the greenhouses of Hausermann's Orchids, Villa Park, Illinois. Below you will find a key that explains how the orchids in this book were titled, as well as definitions of the terms used in each orchid profile.

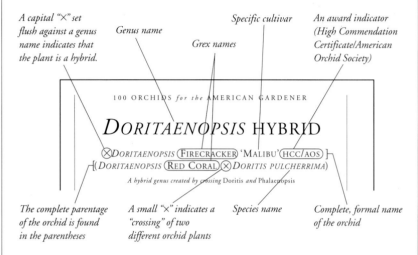

A capital "×" set flush against a genus name indicates that the plant is a hybrid.

Genus name

Grex names

Specific cultivar

An award indicator (High Commendation Certificate/American Orchid Society)

100 ORCHIDS *for the* AMERICAN GARDENER

DORITAENOPSIS HYBRID

⊗*DORITAENOPSIS* (FIRECRACKER) 'MALIBU' (HCC/AOS)
(*DORITAENOPSIS* (RED CORAL) ⊗ *DORITIS PULCHERRIMA*)

A hybrid genus created by crossing Doritis and Phalaenopsis

The complete parentage of the orchid is found in the parentheses

A small "×" indicates a "crossing" of two different orchid plants

Species name

Complete, formal name of the orchid

TYPE indicates whether the orchid is an epiphyte (air plant), terrestrial (earth plant), or lithophyte (rock plant).

GROWTH HABIT indicates whether an orchid is sympodial (moves along by means of a creeping rhizome, producing new growths along the way) or monopodial (having only one growing point that continually increases).

ORIGINS refers to the country or countries where the species or parents of a hybrid were found originally.

BLOOMING SEASON indicates when the orchid is most likely to flower.

LIGHT is indicated as high, medium, low, or a combination (including electric lights).

TEMPERATURE is expressed as cool, intermediate, or warm. Cool is

50º–55ºF, to a maximum of 80ºF; intermediate is 58º–62ºF to 85ºF; and warm is 65º–90ºF.

HUMIDITY is indicated as low, medium, or high average relative humidity. Low refers to below 40 percent (not recommended); medium is about 40–60 percent; high is 60 percent or more.

MOISTURE indicates the degree required in the growing medium, specified by seasons.

GROWING MEDIUM is indicated as A, B, C, or a combination. See pages 35–37.

FERTILIZER regimes are recommended as specifically as possible according to frequency and season.

PLANT SHOWN specifies in which season the plant was photographed and the size pot in which it was blooming.

AERIDES MULTIFLORA

Genus name is from the Greek aer *(air) and* eides *(resembling)*

Characterized by stiff, leathery leaves in two ranks, a healthy *Aerides multiflora* can be sculpturally beautiful in all seasons. When in bloom, however, the flowers are often packed along a descending raceme, which makes for a remarkable display. The sweetly scented flowers bloom in spring or summer and may be purple or nearly white, with purplish spots and tips.

These potentially large, erect, or pendulous plants start to bloom when under a foot tall. Their leaf span, tip to tip, is between 12 and 18 inches.

This orchid looks its finest in a hanging container or set on an overturned clay pot, assuring that the developing spike can grow downward and hang freely. Keep the plant facing one way so the leaves grow in opposite directions.

Aerides are best disturbed as little as possible. In fact, it's not unusual to see smaller pots or wooden baskets merely placed inside larger transplanting containers with fresh medium filling the space between.

The variety *lobbii* has larger flowers in greater numbers than the species itself. Related species requiring similar care include *A. crassifolia* (purple, summer), *A. falcata* (white and rose, summer), *A. houlletiana* (yellow-brown, cream, and magenta, spring), and *A. odorata* var. *lawrenceae* (white and lavender, late spring to early fall).

TYPE: Epiphyte

GROWTH HABIT: Monopodial

ORIGINS: Tropical Himalayas, India to Thailand, Indochina

BLOOMING SEASON: Spring–summer

LIGHT: Medium to high; outdoors, in direct sun for up to half a day; indoors in a sunny window

TEMPERATURE: Intermediate to warm, with a nighttime minimum of 60°F

HUMIDITY: High, with fresh air circulation

MOISTURE: Water freely in warm weather, moderately at other times; avoid protracted or extreme dryness

GROWING MEDIUM: A

FERTILIZER: Spring–summer

PLANT SHOWN: Blooming in spring in a 6-inch pot

*Aerides
multiflora*

ANGRAECUM HYBRID

ANGRAECUM LEONIS × SELF

*Genus name is from a Malayan word (*angurek*) for "orchids with aerial roots"*

This medium-size seedling resulted from crossing the species with itself in order to produce greater vigor than is exhibited by the parent species. Such progeny may also show variation toward smaller or larger leaves and flowers.

This orchid is readily managed in a home collection. The waxy, snowy-white flowers appear in winter or spring and are deliciously scented. They hold up well for a month or more. The one- to seven-flowered inflorescence originates below the leaves. Careful staking of the upright and often numerous stalks, which grow up to a foot long, helps show off individual flowers. (In the specimen pictured, the individual flowers are up to 4 inches across.)

The most famous member of this family is winter-flowering *Angraecum sesquipedale*, discovered by Aubert du Petit Thouars in East Madagascar and described by him in 1822. Subsequently, Charles Darwin deduced that owing to the foot-long, nectar-containing spur, it would have to be pollinated by an unusual moth with an equally long proboscis. His prediction proved true and the hawkmoth responsible was named *Xanthopan morganii praedicta*. Mericlones of one of its progeny, *A*. Veitchii 'White Star' (*A. sesquipedale* × *A. eburneum*), are now widely available and are easy to grow and to flower.

Also noteworthy: *A*. Longiscott (*A. superbum* × *A. scottianum*), which has fragrant white flowers in fall or winter.

TYPE: Epiphyte

GROWTH HABIT: Monopodial

ORIGINS: Madagascar, Comoros Islands

BLOOMING SEASON: Winter–spring

LIGHT: Medium to high; outdoors, in direct sun for up to half a day; indoors in a sunny window, or under multiple fluorescents or high-intensity light

TEMPERATURE: Intermediate, with a nighttime minimum of 60°

HUMIDITY: High, with fresh air circulation

MOISTURE: Water freely in warm weather, moderately at other times

GROWING MEDIUM: A

FERTILIZER: Spring–summer

PLANT SHOWN: Blooming in spring in an 8-inch pot

Angraecum
hybrid

ASCOCENDA HYBRID

×*ASCOCENDA* (*VANDA COERULESCENS* × ×*ASCOCENDA* AROONSRI BEAUTY)

A hybrid genus combining Vanda *and* Ascocentrum

The flowers, leaves, and plant size of this seedling of ×*Ascocenda* are in perfect proportion to each other and are a big part of its appeal for indoor display. This is an outstanding orchid for any collection.

The ×*Ascocenda* hybrid blends the large blue flowers of the *Vanda* with the diminished plant size of the *Ascocentrum.* The plants are easy to grow and often bloom two times a year. Because of beauty, performance, and availability, the name *Ascocenda* has become so popular that growers often forget it's a hybrid genus and in writing may omit the "×" preceding the genus.

Individual flowers grow to about 2 inches across and form a spike of several to many blooms (depending on the age and vigor of the plant), which can stand above the leaves 12 to 18 inches high. Each blossom lasts for several weeks, and it's not unusual for a spike to provide color for two months or more. The leaves, in even ranks, measure 8 to 12 inches wide and grow to similar height.

TYPE: Epiphyte

GROWTH HABIT: Monopodial

ORIGINS: Himalayas to Borneo, Burma, Thailand

BLOOMING SEASON: Winter–spring

LIGHT: Abundant sun; outdoors, may need light shading at midday in hottest weather; indoors in a sunny window, or under multiple fluorescents or high-intensity light

TEMPERATURE: Intermediate to warm, with a winter nighttime minimum of 60°F

HUMIDITY: Above 50% is best, always with good air movement

MOISTURE: Water abundantly during spring and summer, somewhat less in fall and winter.

GROWING MEDIUM: A

FERTILIZER: Heavily during spring and summer, less in fall and winter, depending on light and temperature

PLANT SHOWN: Blooming in spring in a 4-inch pot

Ascocenda
hybrid

ASCOCENDA HYBRID

×*ASCOCENDA* YIP SUM WAH × BANGKOK BLUE

A garden hybrid intermediate between the parents, Ascocentrum × Vanda

Orchids called ×*Ascocenda* were not introduced until 1949, yet their unprecedented beauty and superior growing performance have vaulted them to widespread popularity. It's impossible to have one and not want more in many vivid and hauntingly blended colors.

×*Ascocenda* hybrids are a fortuitous combination of both parents' most admirable features: the relatively small, compact plant of *Ascocentrum* with the large flower of the *Vanda*. Many amateurs succeed in getting bloom twice yearly, and the flowers last perfectly on the plants for up to six weeks.

The first listed parent of this mericloned plant is Yip Sum Wah (*Vanda* Pukele × *Ascocentrum curvifolium*), which is already one of the best known orchids in the world, both for its dominance in ×*Ascocenda* development and for capturing more awards than any other orchid hybrid. To the hybrid shown it gives general family strength, perfect flower shape, and glistening colors. Bangkok Blue, the other parent, is from a cross of Diane Ogawa (Hilo Blue × Sanderana) × *Vanda coerulea.*

TYPE: Epiphyte

GROWTH HABIT: Monopodial

ORIGINS: Himalayas, Burma, China, Thailand

BLOOMING SEASON: Winter–summer

LIGHT: Medium to high; outdoors, in direct sun for half a day or more; indoors in a sunny window, or under multiple fluorescents or high-intensity light

TEMPERATURE: Intermediate to warm, with a nighttime minimum 60°F

HUMIDITY: Medium to high, with good air circulation

MOISTURE: Water freely in all seasons, a little less during the coolest, shortest days of the year (unless under lights)

GROWING MEDIUM: A (use extra-coarse mix)

FERTILIZER: Freely, in all seasons

PLANT SHOWN: Blooming in spring in a 6-inch pot

Ascocenda
hybrid

ASCOCENDA HYBRID

✕*ASCOCENDA* HYBRID Z11947

A hybrid genus combining Vanda *and* Ascocentrum

The plant shown is a perfect example of why the ✕*Ascocenda* orchid has become one of the favored darlings of the orchid world in the second half of the 20th century. The foliage—handsomely symmetrical and sculptural—provides an ideal setting for the compact, upright spike, which is densely set with richly colored, 2-inch flowers. Moreover, the show from one spike can last for eight weeks or more, and the vigorous plants, if adequately fertilized, can be expected to bloom twice yearly.

One way to display this orchid is to set the pot on top of another, overturned pot of the same size or slightly larger. (If the plant is growing in a 6-inch clay pot, for example, set it on an overturned, standard, 6- to 8-inch clay pot.) Position it in relation to a table or floor lamp to light it in the most flattering way possible, and the jewel tones of the flowers will practically sparkle.

The *Ascocentrum* parentage provides the genes for small, tidy plant size, while the *Vanda* side of the hybrid adds a rich and varied color palette: unusual blues and complimentary sunset or autumn hues, apricot, pumpkin, persimmon, even smoky. Seen up close in bright, diffused light or with the sun's rays backlighting the flowers, there may also be a discernible jewellike effect reminiscent of metallic paint.

TYPE: Epiphyte

GROWTH HABIT: Monopodial

ORIGINS: Himalayas to Borneo, Burma, Thailand

BLOOMING SEASON: Winter–summer

LIGHT: High to medium; outdoors, may need light shading at midday; indoors in sunny window, or under multiple fluorescents or high-intensity light

TEMPERATURE: Intermediate to warm, with a winter nighttime minimum of 60°F

HUMIDITY: Medium to high, with good air circulation

MOISTURE: Water freely in all seasons, a little less during the coolest, shortest days of the year (except under lights)

GROWING MEDIUM: A (use extra-coarse mix)

FERTILIZER: All seasons, freely

PLANT SHOWN: Blooming in summer in a 6-inch pot

Ascocenda
hybrid

ASCOCENTRUM AMPULLACEUM

Genus name is from the Greek ascos *(bag) and* kentron *(spur),
referring to the little bagged spur at the base of the lip*

These compact, sculptural plants are ideal for the grower who has limited space or a particular appreciation for the diminutive. Despite their small size, the flowers can be quite showy, facing as they do in all directions and opening wide as if to call attention to themselves.

Since young plants often flower in 2- to 3-inch starter clay pots—and stay fresh for weeks if not a month or more—they are perfect for display on a nightstand within the circle of brightest light cast by a small table lamp. Prolong the duration of bloom by making sure that the roots don't dry excessively at any time. If you slip the growing pot inside a slightly larger cachepot, take care that no water is left standing in the bottom.

Gardeners in the moist tropics and subtropics usually grow *Ascocentrum* in shallow baskets or bulb pans to assure adequate aeration and to prevent the possible water stagnation that could occur in the recesses of deeper containers.

Equally appealing to the home grower are 6-inch-tall *A. curvifolium* (purple to red-orange; spring) and 4-inch-tall *A. miniatum* (orange to red; spring or at almost any season). The genus as a whole figures prominently, along with *Vanda,* in the creation of the showy ✕*Ascocenda* hybrids.

TYPE: Epiphyte

GROWTH HABIT: Monopodial

ORIGINS: Tropical Himalayas, Burma, Thailand

BLOOMING SEASON: Spring

LIGHT: Medium to high; outdoors, in sun for half a day or more; indoors in a sunny window, or under multiple fluorescents or high-intensity light

TEMPERATURE: Intermediate to warm, and never below 60°F

HUMIDITY: High, in air that circulates freely

MOISTURE: Water freely in warm weather, moderately at other times

GROWING MEDIUM: A

FERTILIZER: Spring–summer

PLANT SHOWN: Blooming in late spring in a 4-inch pot

*Ascocentrum
ampullaceum*

ASCOFINETIA HYBRID

×*ASCOFINETIA* PEACHES × *VANDA CRISTATA*

A garden hybrid resulting from crossing Ascocentrum × Neofinetia × Vanda cristata

Connoisseurs are drawn to this unusual orchid (its unique conformation and understated beauty notwithstanding) because it represents three different genera: *Ascocentrum, Neofinetia,* and the so-called *Vanda cristata* (now known officially as *Trudelia cristata*). The slender, leathery leaves can be sinuous and suggestive of movement, like that of a graceful dancer momentarily airborne. The strong air roots are silvery gray except for the emerald tips.

The complex hybrid shown recalls the flower color of *Ascocentrum ampullaceum* and something of the flower shape of a *Neofinetia.* The plant has a certain toughness about it that suggests a tolerance for dry seasons—which are best avoided. The slender leaves recall terete- or semiterete-leaved vanda-like orchids belonging to the genera *Papilionanthe* and *Holcoglossum.*

All these orchids thrive on high light levels outdoors. The more terete-leaved are typically seen in tropical gardens in positions where they receive sufficient sun to produce yellowish-green foliage. In order to prevent outright sunburn, free and abundant air circulation is imperative.

Trudelia cristata, from Nepal to Bhutan, has small green flowers with a maroon-striped, two-pronged lip. Blooms appear in spring at the onset of the main growing season.

TYPE: Epiphyte

GROWTH HABIT: Monopodial

ORIGINS: Himalayas, Burma, China, Japan, Thailand

BLOOMING SEASON: Spring–summer

LIGHT: High to medium; outdoors, in high light; indoors in a sunny window, or under multiple fluorescents or high-intensity light

TEMPERATURE: Intermediate to warm, with a minimum of 60°F

HUMIDITY: Medium to high, in good air circulation

MOISTURE: Water freely all year, somewhat less during the shortest, coolest days of fall and winter, unless sited in an electrically lighted garden

GROWING MEDIUM: A (preferably extra coarse)

FERTILIZER: Freely in spring–summer, less in fall–winter (except under lights)

PLANT SHOWN: Blooming in early summer in a 6-inch pot

Ascofinetia
hybrid

ASPASIA LUNATA

Genus name is possibly from the Greek aspasios *(glad, delightful);*
more likely named to honor Aspasia, the Athenian wife of Pericles

This Brazilian-born orchid blooms in winter or spring and responds favorably to the same care as that of *Oncidium*. The individual flowers are 2 to 3 inches across, with a purple-throated white lip and brown-banded green tepals. They tend to appear among the leaves and might be overlooked in a large collection—but not by the amateur, who will find this an easy orchid to please, and vice versa.

According to current authority, there are five species of *Aspasia* (possibly a sixth that's obscure, although numerous references boost the number to between eight and ten). In its natural range, from Nicaragua to Brazil, *Aspasia* is often found growing epiphytically in trees on branches overhanging rivers. In cultivation, this translates to a need in spring and summer for dappled light; shade against hot, direct sun; abundant moisture; and high humidity. During the fall and early winter, cooler conditions are in order, along with a gradual decline in moisture to ripen new growth.

Botanically, *Aspasia* is allied to *Brassia* and *Miltonia*. The summer-flowering *A. epidendroides* (Central America and Colombia), which grows to about 18 inches tall, has smaller but similarly colored flowers and a light, lemony fragrance. The species with the largest flowers is *A. principissa* (Costa Rica and Panama), which blooms in late winter and spring. Only slightly smaller is *A. variegata* (Costa Rica and Panama), which is similar in color to the others and lightly lemon-scented.

TYPE: Epiphyte

GROWTH HABIT: Sympodial

ORIGINS: Tropical America

BLOOMING SEASON: Winter–spring

LIGHT: Medium; outdoors in dappled light, shaded against direct sun; indoors in a partly sunny window or fluorescent-light garden, or under high-intensity light

TEMPERATURE: Intermediate to warm, with a nighttime minimum of 60°F

HUMIDITY: Medium to high, with good air movement

MOISTURE: Evenly moist to slightly dry

GROWING MEDIUM: A; may also be mounted on bark

FERTILIZER: Spring–summer

PLANT SHOWN: Blooming in spring in a 5-inch pot

*Aspasia
lunata*

BRASSAVOLA NODOSA

(LADY OF THE NIGHT)

Genus named for Antonio Musa Brassavola,
a 16th-century Venetian nobleman and botanist

Until meristemming made many different orchids more commonly available, this great beginner orchid was often the indoor gardener's first venture beyond begonias, geraniums (*Pelargonium* spp.), gardenias, and florist's gloxinias (*Sinningia speciosa*). It adapts easily to pot culture, hanging containers, or mounting on bark.

The pseudobulbs are so slender that they seem hardly more than thickened stems, and the cylindrical leaves are nearly terete. The large, almost heart-shaped lip measures about 2 inches across, with pronounced, slender, spidery tepals. They give off a pervasive honey-sweet vanilla fragrance from early evening until after midnight. The exquisite perfume is often the grower's first sign that *Brassavola nodosa* has come into bloom.

The genus *Brassavola* contains about 15 species, all tropical American. It is most closely allied to *Laelia* and was first described in 1813. Other species favored in cultivation include *B. cordata* (pale green tepals, white lip; summer–fall), *B. cucullata* (pendant leaves, 8 to 18 inches long; spidery greenish to straw-colored flowers with a fringed lip; summer–winter), and *B. fragrans* (tepals yellowish-white, faintly purple-spotted, the white lip having a green spot at the base; summer–fall).

TYPE: Epiphyte or lithophyte

GROWTH HABIT: Sympodial

ORIGINS: Tropical America from Mexico and the West Indies to Peru and Argentina

BLOOMING SEASON: Almost any time

LIGHT: Medium to high; outdoors, in about half a day of sun; indoors in a sunny window, or under multiple fluorescents or high-intensity light

TEMPERATURE: Intermediate to warm, with a minimum of 60°F

HUMIDITY: Medium to high, always with free air movement

MOISTURE: Water abundantly during active growth, less after flowering or in cooler temperatures; do not permit medium to become so dry as to shrivel the the leaves

GROWING MEDIUM: A; may also be mounted on bark

FERTILIZER: Spring–summer; possibly at other times in a light garden

PLANT SHOWN: Blooming in early summer in a 5-inch pot

Brassavola
nodosa

BRASSIA HYBRID

BRASSIA ARANIA VERDE 'STILETTO' × *BRASSIA*
ARCUIGERA 'DARKEST'

Genus named for 19th-century British botanical illustrator William Brass

Most *Brassia* orchids are good confidence builders for beginners. The hybrid shown is typical of this incredibly exotic-appearing genus, which currently enjoys widespread popularity. It's not unusual for healthy, mature plants to flower twice yearly, and for the long inflorescences to last upwards of two months, often giving off a delicious scent. They are available in bloom at reasonable prices and are often seen gracing the rooms featured in shelter magazines.

There are about 30 species, and since many of them have long, spidery tepals, they are commonly known as spider orchids. Brassias are pollinated by wasps, and it's hypothesized that the spider-seeking insects are attracted to the look of the flowers.

The species *B. arcuigera* was first flowered in cultivation in England in 1868 and is still traded as *B. longissima* or *B. lawrenceana* var. *longissima*. It has much larger flowers than *B. lawrenceana,* but is similar. *B. verrucosa* is a large, vigorous plant with pale yellow-green flowers that are 7 or 8 inches long, strikingly arranged in a precise row along a horizontal inflorescence.

TYPE: Epiphyte

GROWTH HABIT: Sympodial

ORIGINS: Costa Rica, Panama, Peru

BLOOMING SEASON: Spring–summer

LIGHT: Medium to high; outdoors, in a little less sun than for cattleyas; indoors in a sunny window, or under multiple fluorescents or high-intensity light

TEMPERATURE: Intermediate, with a nighttime minimum of 60°F

HUMIDITY: Medium to high, with good air circulation

MOISTURE: Keep moist during spring and summer, less so while resting, but never so dry as to cause the pseudobulbs to shrivel

GROWING MEDIUM: A; do not repot unless the medium is beginning to break down

FERTILIZER: Spring–summer

PLANT SHOWN: Blooming in summer in an 8-inch pot

Brassia
hybrid

BRASSOCATTLEYA HYBRID

×*BRASSOCATTLEYA* BINOSA 'WABASH VALLEY' AM/AOS
(*BRASSAVOLA NODOSA* × *CATTLEYA BICOLOR*)

A hybrid genus combining Brassavola *(and/or* Rhyncholaelia*) and* Cattleya

The unusual combination of green tepals and a large, rounded magenta-decorated white lip makes this orchid an arresting sight, sufficiently different to stand out even in the company of other breathtaking orchids. It's a stunning, very fragrant mix of the Brazilian *Cattleya bicolor* and the compact, free-flowering *Brassavola nodosa*. It inherits magenta lips from its *Cattleya* parent and puts forth up to seven blossoms per inflorescence, which may last four to six weeks.

'Wabash Valley,' the cultivar shown, blooms naturally in winter but may also appear in the fall, depending on the individual plant and the conditions under which it's growing. This vigorous plant proliferates sufficiently so that it can be divided after three or four seasons, and makes an excellent acquisition for beginning and intermediate collectors.

The ×*Brassocattleya* hybrid was artificially created for the first time in 1889, but the *Brassavola* × *Cattleya* pairing can also take place unassisted in nature. If a plant purchased in bud is slow to open its flowers, try increasing the amount of light it receives.

TYPE: Epiphyte, lithophyte

GROWTH HABIT: Sympodial

ORIGINS: Tropical America

BLOOMING SEASON: winter

LIGHT: Medium to high; outdoors, in about half a day of sun; indoors in a sunny window, or under multiple fluorescents or high-intensity light

TEMPERATURE: Moderate, with a winter nighttime minimum of 55°–60°F

HUMIDITY: Medium to high, with excellent air movement

MOISTURE: Let dry between waterings, but never to the point of shriveling the pseudobulbs

GROWING MEDIUM: A

FERTILIZER: Usually spring–summer, during periods of active growth

PLANT SHOWN: Blooming in fall in a 5-inch pot

Brassocattleya
hybrid

BRASSOLAELIOCATTLEYA HYBRID

×*BRASSOLAELIOCATTLEYA*
HAUSERMANN'S HOLIDAY 'ISHPEMING'

Trigeneric genus created in 1897 by crossing Brassavola × Laelia × Cattleya

This is a quintessential orchid of its type, possessed of flowers that are as generous to the nose as they are to the eyes. They give off an abundance of fragrance at all hours: sweet, sultry, honey, vanilla, a steamy greenhouse filled with exotic blooms on a frigid day. It can buckle the knees.

This orchid is described as unifoliate, meaning that one leaf grows from each pseudobulb (rather than two, as in many closely related orchids that are bifoliate). An established 'Ishpeming' can have upward of a dozen vigorous growths. Each pseudobulb and leaf unit stands 15 to 18 inches tall, composed of nearly 60 percent foliage, the rest being the large, elongated pseudobulb, which has a papery, netted sheath. The flowers can measure to 8 inches across. Tepals and petals are a silvery-rosy-lavender (many consider this *the* orchid color), and the much-ruffled lip is a more intense shade of the same color, with added glowing yellow blotches and veining in the throat. Blooms last about a week in water and up to six weeks on the plant.

TYPE: Epiphyte

GROWTH HABIT: Sympodial

ORIGINS: Tropical America

BLOOMING SEASON: Fall–early winter

LIGHT: Medium to high; outdoors, with sufficient filtering of direct rays to avoid sunburn; indoors in a sunny window, or under multiple fluorescents or high-intensity light

TEMPERATURE: Intermediate, with a winter nighttime minimum of 55°–60°F

HUMIDITY: Medium to high, with good air circulation

MOISTURE: Water generously during spring and summer, allowing to dry a bit between waterings; less in fall and winter, but never allow to become so dry as to shrivel the pseudobulbs

GROWING MEDIUM: A

FERTILIZER: Lightly, frequently during spring and summer, less in fall and winter

PLANT SHOWN: Blooming in fall in a 7-inch pot

Brassolaeliocattleya hybrid

BRASSOLAELIOCATTLEYA
HYBRID

×*BRASSOLAELIOCATTLEYA*
MARTEN HAUSERMANN 'ADDISON SPLASH'

Trigeneric genus created in 1897 by crossing Brassavola × Laelia × Cattleya

'Addison Splash' is one of the newly popular "splash" cattleya-type orchids, which will typically be found listed in catalogs among the "art shades and novelty colors." The spectacular splashing of the lip color across the petals of these orchids gives them an exotic appearance—and their name. They possess an easy culture, adapting well to the care that can be given by a home grower.

'Addison Splash' produces up to four or five large flowers, each 6 to 8 inches across, per inflorescence. The stem is held strongly above the unifoliate pseudobulbs (each having but one leaf, although an established plant will have several growths at once) that stand 15 to 18 inches tall. The floral parts have crimped and ruffled edgings, and the flowers freely emit the rich honey-vanilla "orchid" fragrance. (As not all fragrant roses give the "true rose" scent, so it is with orchids, which give off many different scents.) The flowers last about a week in water and up to six weeks on the plant.

TYPE: Epiphyte

GROWTH HABIT: Sympodial

ORIGINS: Tropical America

BLOOMING SEASON: Fall–early winter

LIGHT: Medium to high; outdoors, with sufficient filtering of direct rays to avoid sunburn; indoors in a sunny window, or under multiple fluorescents or high-intensity light

TEMPERATURE: Intermediate, with a winter nighttime minimum of 55°–60°F

HUMIDITY: Medium to high, with good air circulation

MOISTURE: Generously during spring and summer, but drying a bit between waterings; less in fall and winter, but never allow to become so dry as to shrivel the pseudobulbs

GROWING MEDIUM: A

FERTILIZER: Lightly, frequently during spring and summer, less in fall and winter

PLANT SHOWN: Blooming in fall in a 10-inch pot

Brassolaeliocattleya hybrid

BRASSOLAELIOCATTLEYA HYBRID

✕*BRASSOLAELIOCATTLEYA* SEA SWIRL 'MERMAID'

Trigeneric genus created in 1897 by crossing Brassavola ✕ Laelia ✕ Cattleya

This green mericlone has panache. The large, colorful, ruffled lip stands out enticingly from the pale lime green tepals, altogether displaying a large flower up to 6 inches across or more on a medium to tall plant. Even one or two blooms exude enough fragrance to announce their presence in a room.

It is not likely that any of these pale green flowers will be overlooked or mistaken for leaves, no matter how many other plants may compete for attention. They have a unique beauty that stands out in a crowd.

Sea Swirl 'Mermaid' is a vigorous orchid that can become a confidence builder for the beginning grower. Time spent outdoors in warm weather profits this plant, although a sunny window in an apartment can benefit year-round. It also responds well to being grown under four 40-watt fluorescent tubes placed 6 to 12 inches above the top of the leaves.

The collector of green flowers also may wish to collect Hausermann's Symphony 'Pastoral,' Ports of Paradise 'Emerald Isle' (FCC/AOS), and Sea Swirl 'Whirlpool' (HCC/AOS).

TYPE: Epiphyte

GROWTH HABIT: Sympodial

ORIGINS: Tropical America

BLOOMING SEASON: Summer

LIGHT: Medium to high; outdoors, with sufficient filtering of direct rays to avoid sunburn; indoors in a sunny window, or under multiple fluorescents or high-intensity light

TEMPERATURE: Intermediate, with a winter nighttime minimum of 55°–60°F

HUMIDITY: Medium to high, with good air circulation

MOISTURE: Water generously during spring and summer, drying a bit between waterings; less during fall and winter, but never allow to become so dry as to shrivel the pseudobulbs

GROWING MEDIUM: A

FERTILIZER: Lightly, frequently during spring and summer, less in fall and winter

PLANT SHOWN: Blooming in summer in a 6-inch pot

Brassolaeliocattleya hybrid

CATTLEYA BOB BETTS 'WHITE LIGHTNING'

Genus named for William Cattley (1788–1835),
among the first to grow epiphytic orchids in England

Bob Betts is the result of a cross of Bow Bells × *Cattleya mossiae*. It is, quite possibly, the quintessential big white ruffly cattleya orchid—the sight of which can cause the knees to buckle, the smell of which can bring cries of delight if not outright swooning.

By the time it's five years old, a thrifty cattleya plant like Bob Betts may well occupy a pot between 8 and 10 or 12 inches in diameter, and produce two or more spikes at once, each bearing up to three flowers. If you have experienced the visual and sensual pleasures of these fragrant flowers even once, it's sufficient ever after for the mere thought of one to evoke one of the most alluring of olfactory memories.

Cattleyas such as Bob Betts 'White Lightning' or Mount Hood 'Mary' AM/AOS usually bloom in winter, which is incredibly propitious timing and part of their great appeal to the orchid grower. Since the plants tend to rejuvenate primarily in spring and summer, it's also common for the flowers to make an early appearance. In fact, fall bloom is nearly as likely as winter bloom.

TYPE: Epiphyte, lithophyte
GROWTH HABIT: Sympodial
ORIGINS: Tropical America
BLOOMING SEASON: Winter
LIGHT: Medium to high; outdoors, with some filtering of sun's hottest rays through midday to prevent scorching the leaves; indoors in a sunny window, or under multiple fluorescents or high-intensity light
TEMPERATURE: Moderate, with winter nights no lower than 55°–60°F
HUMIDITY: Medium to high, always with good air movement

MOISTURE: Give ample water; allow plants to dry between waterings, but never to the point of shriveling the pseudobulbs
GROWING MEDIUM: A
FERTILIZER: Generously during spring and summer, little or none in fall and winter
PLANT SHOWN: Blooming in fall in a 10-inch pot

Cattleya Bob Betts
'White Lightning'

CATTLEYA GUATEMALENSIS 'LAKEVIEW'

Genus named for William Cattley (1788–1835),
one of the first to grow epiphytic orchids in England

'Lakeview' is a variety of *Cattleya guatemalensis* that occurs naturally as a hybrid and can also be created in horticulture. The flowers have their own distinct color, an orange coppery pink more associated with hybrid roses than hybrid orchids. Blooming in a 6-inch pot, 'Lakeview' will stand about 18 inches tall and make an outstanding specimen when displayed on a table, console, or credenza.

The small, typically shaped cattleya flowers appear in generous numbers of six or more on an upright inflorescence that stands well above the attractive bifoliate leaves. The individual flowers are vigorous, lasting up to four weeks or more on the plant, and quite well (seven to ten days) when cut.

C. guatemalensis, C. deckeri, and *C. pachecoi* have at times been considered separate species. Botanically speaking, they are considered natural hybrids, members of a hybrid swarm between *C. aurantiaca* and *C. skinneri.*

TYPE: Epiphyte

GROWTH HABIT: Sympodial

ORIGINS: Mexico, Guatemala

BLOOMING SEASON: Spring–summer

LIGHT: Medium to high; outdoors, with enough filtering shade to prevent leaf scorch; indoors in a sunny window, or under multiple fluorescents or high-intensity light

TEMPERATURE: Intermediate to warm, with a winter minimum of 55°–65°F.

HUMIDITY: Medium to high, with good air circulation

MOISTURE: Water generously during spring and summer, with a bit of drying between; less in fall and winter, but never to the extent of shriveling the pseudobulbs; misting may be preferable to watering during the resting season

GROWING MEDIUM: A

FERTILIZER: Regularly during spring and summer, less or not at all in fall and winter

PLANT SHOWN: Blooming in early summer in a 6-inch pot

*Cattleya
guatemalensis*
'Lakeview'

CATTLEYA HYBRID

CATTLEYA BICOLOR 'BURGUNDY' × *CATTLEYA ACLANDIAE* 'SUMMER QUEEN'

Named for William Cattley (1788–1835),
among the first to grow epiphytic orchids in England

In bloom, this fragrant *Cattleya* hybrid seedling is wonderful for enjoying up close—on a bathroom counter, a lamp table, a desk. The plants are conveniently small, usually 12 to 14 inches tall, which makes them manageable in a window or light garden where prime space is at at a premium.

This orchid reveals traits of both species parents in the waxy, fragrant, 4-inch flowers that can last a month or more on small, bifoliate plants. One parent, *Cattleya bicolor,* has green tepals, flushed red-brown, and a purple-red lip. It has long, jointed pseudobulbs 1 to 2 feet tall and is fall-blooming, but may bloom in spring as well. *C. aclandiae,* the other parent, has fragrant yellow-green flowers with dark purple blotches and spots arranged transversely, and a lip that is purple-veined on a bright rose-purple background. Its blooms appear variously at almost any season. Perhaps it's no surprise that the offspring of this mating has produced a seedling that may come into bloom at almost any season.

TYPE: Epiphyte

GROWTH HABIT: Sympodial

ORIGINS: Brazil

BLOOMING SEASON: Spring–summer, or at almost any time of year

LIGHT: Medium to high; outdoors, with enough shade to prevent leaf-scorch; indoors in a sunny window, or under multiple fluorescents or high-intensity light

TEMPERATURE: Intermediate to warm, with a winter nighttime minimum of 55°–65°F

HUMIDITY: Medium to high, with good air circulation

MOISTURE: Water generously during spring and summer, drying a bit between waterings; less so in fall and winter, but never allow to become so dry as to shrivel the pseudobulbs; misting the pseudobulbs during the resting season can be better than actually watering them

GROWING MEDIUM: A

FERTILIZER: Regularly in spring and summer, less or not at all in fall and winter

PLANT SHOWN: Blooming in summer in a 5-inch pot

Cattleya
hybrid

Cattleya HYBRID

Cattleya Bobker's Kaleidoscope × (*Cattleya* brabantiae × *Laeliocattleya* Acker's Madison)

Named for William Cattley (1788–1835),
among the first to grow epiphytic orchids in England

This is a cluster-type *Cattleya* hybrid that produces a generous number of 3- to 4-inch flowers. The tepals are lavender with darker rose-pink spots that match the tip of the mostly white lip. Since the flowers appear on relatively small plants—around 12 inches tall—at any time from fall to spring and last for several weeks, this is a popular and collectible cattleya.

Hybrid vigor is another trait that makes this an outstanding orchid, especially where conditions may not always be ideal or where space is limited. For a relatively small plant, it sends up a generous bouquet of flowers at the top of every healthy, matured new growth from the previous season.

One of the grandparents of the hybrid shown is *C. brabantiae,* which resulted from a cross of *C. aclandiae* × *C. loddigesii,* and was the first *Cattleya* hybrid to win an award—the silver Banksian Medal from England's Royal Horticultural Society in 1863. Another grandparent, an ×*Laeliocattleya,* may technically move this collectible from placement here at *Cattleya* to ×*Laeliocattleya.* The plant shown, however, is as of now sold as a *Cattleya* hybrid.

TYPE: Epiphyte

GROWTH HABIT: Sympodial

ORIGINS: Tropical America

BLOOMING SEASON: Fall–spring

LIGHT: Medium to high; outdoors, with enough shade to prevent leaf scorch; indoors in a sunny window, or under multiple fluorescents or high-intensity light

TEMPERATURE: Intermediate to warm, with a winter nighttime minimum of 55°–65°F

HUMIDITY: Medium to high, with good air circulation

MOISTURE: Water generously during spring and summer, less in fall and winter, but never allow to become so dry as to shrivel the pseudobulbs

GROWING MEDIUM: A

FERTILIZER: Generously in spring and summer, little or none in fall and winter

PLANT SHOWN: Blooming in late winter in a 5-inch pot

Cattleya
hybrid

CATTLEYA LABIATA 'AUTUMNALIS'

To many people, this is the quintessential orchid. It also happens to be the species on which the genus *Cattleya* was founded. If you're building an orchid collection, this plant should be among your first acquisitions. And if your goal is continuous bloom all year long, *C. labiata* 'Autumnalis' is well equipped to do its share in the fall.

The sweetly perfumed, medium-large, long-lasting flowers range in color from rose-violet to lavender, with a ruffled dark magenta lip margined in pale mauve. The inner throat is mottled yellow and sometimes streaked with purple.

One of the desirable traits *C. labiata* has passed along to its progeny is the quality of its petals and sepals. Contained within their often delicate colors are sparkling or luminous cells. Seen up close in flattering light, these are among nature's most easily admired flowers.

Although this species no longer appears in the Organ Mountains of Brazil, where it was discovered, it is found in ample quantity in eastern Brazil. There is an all-white form, *C. labiata* var. *alba,* and another, *C. labiata* var. *cooksoniae,* which has white petals and sepals with a crimson lip.

TYPE: Epiphyte

GROWTH HABIT: Sympodial

ORIGINS: Eastern Brazil

BLOOMING SEASON: Fall

LIGHT: Medium to high (blooms more enthusiastically in greater light); outdoors, in up to half a day of sun; indoors in a sunny window, or under multiple fluorescents or high-intensity light; leaves may develop a reddish edge to indicate they are receiving their upper limit of light

TEMPERATURE: Moderate to warm, with a minimum wintertime temperature of 50°–55°F

HUMIDITY: Medium to high, with good air circulation

MOISTURE: Plenty of water during period of active growth; less after the new pseudobulbs are fully grown; misting can be preferable to watering during the resting season

GROWING MEDIUM: A

FERTILIZER: Regularly in spring and summer, less or not at all after the new pseudobulbs are fully grown

PLANT SHOWN: Blooming in fall in a 5-inch pot

*Cattleya
labiata*
'Autumnalis'

CATTLEYA WALKERIANA VAR. ALBA 'PENDENTIVE' AM/AOS

Named for William Cattley (1788–1835),
among the first to grow epiphytic orchids in England

This hybrid is treasured for its unusually waxy, fragrant white flowers that grow up to 6 inches across and last for up to a month. The short, compact plants grow to only 12 inches tall, which is always a popular trait with orchid collectors.

At first glance, 'Pendentive' might be mistaken as nothing more than another white cattleya. Closer inspection reveals a graceful flower that's taller than it is wide. The formation of the lip in the context of its tepals and petals suggests a figure, perhaps an angel, all robed in white.

Fortunately, 'Pendentive,' which has received the Award of Merit from the American Orchid Society, has been meristemmed so that vigorous young plants, soon-to-bloom, can be purchased for a reasonable sum. For the collector in need of a large white, fragrant flower to appreciate up close in summer, hardly any other in the floral kingdom equals 'Pendentive.'

TYPE: Epiphyte

GROWTH HABIT: Sympodial

ORIGINS: Species is from Brazil

BLOOMING SEASON: Winter–spring

LIGHT: Medium to high; outdoors, with enough filtering shade to prevent leaf scorch; indoors in a sunny window, or under multiple fluorescents or high-intensity light

TEMPERATURE: Intermediate to warm, with a winter nighttime minimum of 55°–65°F

HUMIDITY: Medium to high, with good air circulation

MOISTURE: Water generously during spring and summer, less in fall and winter, but never allow to become so dry as to shrivel the pseudobulbs; misting can be preferable to watering during the resting season

GROWING MEDIUM: A

FERTILIZER: Regularly in spring and summer, less or not at all in fall and winter

PLANT SHOWN: Blooming in spring in a 5-inch pot

Cattleya walkeriana
var. *alba* 'Pendentive'
AM/AOS

CATTLEYTONIA HYBRID

× *CATTLEYTONIA* WHY NOT ×
× *CATTLEYTONIA* WHY NOT

A hybrid genus crossing Broughtonia *and* Cattleya

The hybrid genus × *Cattleytonia* bears rounded, full flowers in bright, clear colors. Typically, it's a cross of *Broughtonia sanguinea* and one of any number of different species and variants of *Cattleya.* Why Not, the hybrid shown here, is considered an unusually successful combination of genes from two illustrious family trees.

The color of Why Not's flowers recalls *Cattleya aurantiaca,* a Mexican bifoliate, which has been used in breeding to introduce orange and red to the primarily purple *Cattleya* palette. Another desirable trait passed along by this species to × *Cattleytonia* is the ability of young plants to bloom with relative ease at almost any season from fall to spring. The reddish orange flowers of this hybrid span up to 3 inches across, and are borne at 12 to 15 inches in height, slightly above the unifoliate pseudobulbs that eventually form quite a handsome foliage mass.

× *Cattleytonia* plants need more light than the average *Cattleya,* on the order of that given to sun-loving *Broughtonia.* Except in climates given to mostly cloudy weather, × *Cattleytonia* can be grown outdoors in adequate sun all through the warm weather. At other seasons, it can be carried along in a window that receives at least half a day of sun, or in a situation that might combine daylight and a bank of fluorescents, or exposure to high-intensity light at night and on overcast days.

TYPE: Epiphyte

GROWTH HABIT: Sympodial

ORIGINS: Tropical America

BLOOMING SEASON: Fall–winter

LIGHT: Medium to high; outdoors, shield from direct sun at midday; indoors in a sunny window, or under multiple fluorescents or high-intensity light

TEMPERATURE: Medium to high, with a winter nighttime minimum of 55°–65°F

HUMIDITY: High, with good air circulation

MOISTURE: Water generously, then permit to dry slightly before dousing again

GROWING MEDIUM: A

FERTILIZER: Spring and summer, little or none during fall and winter

PLANT SHOWN: Blooming in fall in a 3-inch pot

Cattleytonia
hybrid

COCHLEANTHES DISCOLOR

Genus name is from the Greek kochlos *(shell) and* anthos *(flower),*
for the shell-like shape of the lip

This obscure orchid's stock-in-trade is that at some stages the lightly scented flowers come as close to blue as can be found in the family. The spreading outer lobe of the lip is where the strongest blue-violet coloring occurs. In the more narrow tepals, the color is much paler, sometimes to the palest violet or even a faint creamy green at times.

The flowers of *Cochleanthes discolor* are about 2 inches in diameter. They appear singly on short stems from a point at the base of the leaves, often in such numbers as to appear crowded. The pseudobulbs, 1 to 2 inches tall, give rise to relatively thin, textured leaves 1½ inches wide by 6 inches long.

Altogether, the genus *Cochleanthes* contains nine species found widely dispersed in the American tropics. The flowers of *C. aromatica* are perhaps a bit showier—larger than those of *C. discolor*—yet they are less likely to reveal a bluish tint. In *C. marginata,* the pink flower in winter is reminiscent of a small cattleya.

The genus *Cochleanthes* was first described in 1836. However, its species have often been placed in either *Zygopetalum* or *Warscewiczella,* despite the fact that botanically, *Cochleanthes* is more closely allied with the little-known genera *Chondrorhyncha* and *Huntleya. Cochleanthes discolor* is still offered in the trade as *Warscewiczella discolor,* and the earliest description, by John Lindley in 1849, gives yet another name: *Warrea discolor.*

TYPE: Epiphyte

GROWTH HABIT: Sympodial

ORIGINS: Cuba, Honduras, Costa Rica, Panama, Venezuela

BLOOMING SEASON: Spring–fall

LIGHT: Medium; outdoors, in dappled shade; indoors in a partly shaded window or fluorescent-light garden

TEMPERATURE: Intermediate to cool, but avoid temperatures higher than 80°–85°F

HUMIDITY: High, with good air circulation

MOISTURE: Evenly moist to slightly dry; avoid extremes

GROWING MEDIUM: A, with good drainage; best in hanging baskets or pots

FERTILIZER: Lightly, frequently, consistently in spring and summer

PLANT SHOWN: Blooming in summer in a 6-inch pot

*Cochleanthes
discolor*

COLMANARA HYBRID

✕*COLMANARA* WILDCAT
(*MILTONIA* ✕ *ODONTOGLOSSUM* ✕ *ONCIDIUM*)

A hybrid genus named for Sir Jeremiah Colman (1859–1942), of the mustard firm
Colman & Sons, who was known for having a huge collection of orchids

Wildcat is a 1992 hybrid (*Odontonia* Rustic Bridge ✕ *Odontocidium* Crowborough) descended from *Miltoniopsis Oncidium,* and *Odontoglossum* grandparents. The *Ondontoglossum* orchid prefers cool conditions, and *Oncidium* is suited to an intermediate to warm range. The resulting cross (including *Miltoniopsis,* once known as *Miltonia*) is an outstanding plant that is slightly more tolerant of warm temperatures, but not much above 80°F.

The Wildcat plant grows 18 to 20 inches tall, producing a fairly upright inflorescence to 36 inches tall with up to 50 flowers, each growing to 3 inches across. The tepals glow deep gold with mahogany splotches; the lip is reminiscent of the mask on a *Miltoniopsis* flower—white to pale pink with dark, velvety red markings. Although the primary bloom season is late summer through fall, flowering may occur at any time of year.

Meristemming has made Wildcat and other ✕*Colmanara* hybrids available almost overnight. Easy to grow and outstanding in appearance, they have become popular in the world of orchid hobbyists yet are strangely absent from all but the most recent growing guides.

TYPE: Epiphyte

GROWTH HABIT: Sympodial

ORIGINS: Original species from subtropical and tropical America

BLOOMING SEASON: Late summer–fall or winter–spring

LIGHT: Medium; outdoors, with sufficient shade to prevent leaf scorch; indoors near a sunny to partly sunny window, or under multiple fluorescents or high-intensity light

TEMPERATURE: Intermediate, with a winter minimum of 55°–60°F, and highs of 78°–80°F

HUMIDITY: Medium to high, with good air circulation

MOISTURE: Keep watered all year, permitting slight drying between waterings

GROWING MEDIUM: A

FERTILIZER: Regularly during spring and summer, somewhat less in fall and winter

PLANT SHOWN: Blooming in late spring in a 5-inch pot

Colmanara
hybrid

CYMBIDIUM AVIEMORE 'DECEMBER PINKIE'

Genus name is from the Greek kymbes *(boat-shaped), inspired by the lip*

Although cymbidium flowers like 'December Pinkie' are not expected to be fragrant, this variety gives off an almost imperceptible hint of an old-fashioned flower shop, the type with a greenhouse attached. There is definitely something sweet, earthy, and altogether floral in the fragrance. Commercial cymbidiums used in floristry are not usually fragrant, but there are numerous species that do give rich scent, including *Cymbidium ensifolium, C. goeringii, C. kanran, C. lancifolium, C. parishii, C. sinense,* and *C. tigrinum.*

This compact (for a cymbidium) plant might be considered a miniature form of Pink Giant. The foliage mass—2 to 3 feet across and about 18 inches tall—is impressive, and makes a spectacular show topping a pedestal in a bright to sunny window. The plant shown has two flower spikes, each 18 to 24 inches tall, bearing 18 to 20 flowers that are 2 to 3 inches across. It was photographed in October, after two spikes had already bloomed. A plant of this size may well produce additional spikes by the holiday season; hence the name 'December Pinkie.'

TYPE: Terrestrial

GROWTH HABIT: Sympodial

ORIGINS: Asia, Australia

BLOOMING SEASON: Fall–winter

LIGHT: Medium to high; outdoors or in a bright to sunny window; also possible under multiple fluorescents or high-intensity light

TEMPERATURE: Cool to intermediate, with fall and winter night temperatures of 45°–55°F ideal; chilling—but not a frost—helps set buds

HUMIDITY: Medium to high, always with good air circulation

MOISTURE: Evenly moist, except drier (and cooler) after new growth is complete

GROWING MEDIUM: B

FERTILIZER: Spring and summer; timed-release 14-14-14 works well

PLANT SHOWN: Blooming in fall in a 10-inch pot

Cymbidium
Aviemore
'December
Pinkie'

CYMBIDIUM HYBRID

CYMBIDIUM GOLDEN ELF 'SUNDUST'

Genus name is from the Greek kymbes *(boat-shaped), inspired by the shape of the lip*

This elegant and graceful miniature yellow mericlone has received a High Commendation Certificate from the American Orchid Society. Part of its allure is that it happens to be among the relatively few summer-blooming cymbidiums.

This hybrid came out of a unique cross between the fall-flowering *Cymbidium ensifolium* and 'Enid Haupt.' The former is a small, grassy-leaved species from India and China to the Philippines; the latter is a large-flowered hybrid named for the founder of *Seventeen* magazine and a generous benefactor to the New York Botanical Garden. Enid Haupt was among the first to promote the use of flowering orchid plants for decorating the home.

'Sundust,' like *C. ensifolium*, has very small pseudobulbs that send up grassy leaves in tuft formations; it is truly attractive in all seasons, often blooming the first time in a 4- to 5-inch pot with cheerful yellow flowers that can last up to two months. Miniature cymbidiums like 'Sundust' can look particularly beautiful when displayed in a tall bonsai pot or in an English Long Tom clay pot.

Another outstanding miniature yellow cymbidium is Nonna 'Goldilocks' (a cross of the faintly scented Australian *C. madidum* × Alexanderi), which blooms in the spring. Like 'Sundust,' it has received recognition (The Award of Merit) from the American Orchid Society.

TYPE: Terrestrial

GROWTH HABIT: Sympodial

ORIGINS: Southern China, southeastern Tibet.

BLOOMING SEASON: Summer–early fall

LIGHT: Medium to high; outdoors, in about half a day of sun; indoors in a sunny window, or under high-intensity light

TEMPERATURE: Cool to warm, from a 40°F minimum to an 80°F maximum

HUMIDITY: Medium to high, with good air movement

MOISTURE: Evenly moist except drier (and cooler) after new growth is complete

GROWING MEDIUM: B

FERTILIZER: Spring–summer

PLANT SHOWN: Blooming in summer in a 7-inch pot

Cymbidium
hybrid

CYMBIDIUM PINK GIANT

Genus name is from the Greek kymbes *(boat-shaped), inspired by the lip*

Pink Giant is typical of the large-flowered hybrid commercial cymbidiums that are a mainstay in floristry. The plants grow vigorous, grassy leaves up to 18 inches long, sprouting from big pseudobulbs nearly the size of a goose egg. Spikes of large, waxy flowers soar upwards of 2 feet high and provide a dramatic show for up to three months, usually in fall or winter. The flowers come in nearly every color imaginable, including green, but never purple or even a faint blue.

Individual cut blooms last well and can be kept supplied with water by insertion in a florist's water pick or any bud vase. Spikes can also be cut and enjoyed for weeks if not months in a vase regularly refilled with fresh water.

This type of cymbidium is often used in mild-climate gardens as a landscape plant. It requires a suitably humus-rich, well-drained bed, or it can be cultivated in large pots. Plants established in these ways will not need to be disturbed until the central part of the clump becomes leafless and crowded, usually after several years.

TYPE: Epiphyte, terrestrial

GROWTH HABIT: Sympodial

ORIGINS: Asia, Australia

BLOOMING SEASON: Late fall–early spring

LIGHT: High during active growth period; outdoors in sun, but shaded at midday; indoors in a sunny window, or under multiple fluorescents or high-intensity light

TEMPERATURE: Cool to intermediate, with fall and winter night temperatures of 45°–55°F ideal, and cool enough to set buds

HUMIDITY: Medium to high, with good air circulation

MOISTURE: Evenly moist except drier (and cooler) after new growth is complete

GROWING MEDIUM: B

FERTILIZER: Spring and summer; timed-release 14-14-14 works well

PLANT SHOWN: Blooming in fall in a 10-inch pot

Cymbidium
Pink Giant

CYMBIDIUM PIPETA 'YORK'

Genus name is from the Greek kymbes *(boat-shaped), inspired by the lip*

Cymbidium Pipeta 'York' is a miniature, winter-blooming orchid. Its compact habit and abundance of red blooms makes it special. The plant shown has about 30 flowers on each inflorescence, which grows about 15 to 18 inches tall.

C. pumilum—one of the parents of this hybrid, along with Spartan Queen—has now been reclassified as *C. floribundum.* It's a spring and summer bloomer from southern China and Taiwan. The rusty brown or green-edged yellowish green flowers with a maroon-blotched (rarely pink) lip are packed along an arching raceme 12 to 18 inches long.

Miniature cymbidiums generally make fine houseplants and can also be accommodated in a fluorescent-light garden, provided it has four 40-watt tubes or the equivalent positioned a few inches directly above the foliage. Cymbidiums require a period of chilling in fall to mature the new growth and set the buds.

One of the smallest species in the genus, *C. tigrinum,* grows to 8 inches high. It has greenish beige petals and sepals that surround a bright white lip marked in purple-crimson. Its flowers are 2 to 3½ inches across and grow sparsely on an arching raceme with narrowly elliptical to lance-shaped leaves measuring 3 to 7 inches long and slightly more than an inch across.

TYPE: Epiphyte, terrestrial

GROWTH HABIT: Sympodial

ORIGINS: Southern China, Taiwan

BLOOMING SEASON: Late fall–winter

LIGHT: High during active growth period; outdoors in sun, but shaded at midday; indoors in a sunny window, or under multiple fluorescents or high-intensity light

TEMPERATURE: Cool to intermediate, with winter night temperatures of 45°–55°F ideal, and cool enough to set buds

HUMIDITY: Medium to high, with good air circulation

MOISTURE: Evenly moist except drier (and cooler) after new growth is complete

GROWING MEDIUM: B

FERTILIZER: Spring and summer; timed-release 14-14-14 works well

PLANT SHOWN: Blooming in fall in a 7-inch pot

Cymbidium
Pipeta 'York'

DENDROBIUM EMERALD FANTASY

Genus name is from the Greek dendros *(tree) and* bios *(life)*

Not everyone appreciates green flowers. Among those who do, however, Emerald Fantasy has become a darling, as familiar to some as an 'Envy' zinnia or the gladiolus 'Four Leaf Clover.' Descended from a breeding line for antelope hybrids (so named because they have two upper petals that are slender and twisting toward the top, suggesting a pair of horns), Emerald Fantasy mericlones are typically cultivated in Hawaii and distributed to the world market as soon as the spikes are sufficiently advanced to withstand travel. Quite miraculously, they are able to resume growing in a completely new environment and to produce a remarkable flower show that can last up to two months. The specimen shown doesn't have the pronounced antelope shape of more mature specimens.

A fine example of the "antelope" character may be seen in *D. gouldii,* a fall-blooming species from New Guinea that bears prodigious numbers of yellow-and-brown or white-and-violet-mauve flowers in erect or arching sprays. These displays originate out of the upper nodes along leafy stems to 3 feet tall or more.

TYPE: Ephiphyte

GROWTH HABIT: Sympodial

ORIGINS: Asian and Pacific tropics and subtropics

BLOOMING SEASON: Any

LIGHT: Medium to high; outdoors, in up to half a day of sun; indoors in a sunny window, or under multiple fluorescents or high-intensity light

TEMPERATURE: Intermediate, with a winter low of 50°–60°F; normally cooler temperatures in fall help mature the new growth and set flower buds

HUMIDITY: Medium to high, with constant air movement

MOISTURE: Water freely in spring and summer, less from fall until midwinter, but never allow to become so dry as to cause leaves or canes to shrivel

GROWING MEDIUM: A, with perfect drainage

FERTILIZER: Dilute amounts of 30-10-10 with nearly every watering during spring and summer, changing to 15-30-15 by Labor Day so as to ripen growth and set flower buds

PLANT SHOWN: Blooming in the spring in a 5-inch pot

Dendrobium
Emerald
Fantasy

DENDROBIUM FARMERI

This showy evergreen dendrobium typically grows canelike pseudobulbs 18 to 24 inches tall set with relatively large leaves. The white (or pale lilac-mauve) and primrose-yellow flowers appear in loose sprays, usually in spring or summer, cascading from an upper node and lasting a month or more.

Dendrobium farmeri (along with *D. chrysotoxum, D. densiflorum, D. fimbriatum, D. moschatum,* and *D. thyrsiflorum*) gets on well given cattleya treatment. In fact, this entire group of dendrobiums is easily managed in a greenhouse where cattleyas are featured. They can probably take more sun than the cattleyas (except for *D. moschatum,* which can take a little shade), and may be arranged to take advantage of microclimates for extra light. When they are grouped with more light-sensitive orchids, most dendrobiums can front orchids requiring less light.

In the fall, dendrobiums need night temperatures of around 50°F and regular if light watering to keep the leaves and stemlike pseudobulbs sufficiently well hydrated. Especially during this season, spider mites can be troublesome on the undersides of the leaves. A forceful stream of water will discourage these tiny but potentially devastating insects; in some cases, it may even be prudent to use a miticide against them.

The original collections of *D. farmeri* were from Malaya, where they grew on the branches of large trees overhanging rivers.

TYPE: Epiphyte

GROWTH HABIT: Sympodial

ORIGINS: Himalayas, Burma, Thailand, Vietnam, Malaya

BLOOMING SEASON: Spring and summer

LIGHT: Medium to high; outdoors, in half a day of sun; indoors in a sunny window

TEMPERATURE: Intermediate to warm, with a nighttime minimum of 60°F

HUMIDITY: Medium to high, with good air movement

MOISTURE: Evenly moist, drier in fall to early winter, but never so dry as to cause pseudobulbs to shrivel

GROWING MEDIUM: A

FERTILIZER: Spring–summer

PLANT SHOWN: Blooming in summer in an 8-inch pot

*Dendrobium
farmeri*

DENDROBIUM HYBRID

DENDROBIUM KEIKI BELL × LADY CHARM

Genus name is from the Greek dendros *(tree) and* bios *(life)*

Keiki Bell × Lady Charm has an impressive family tree, which is not surprising when you consider this popular orchid's rich, velvety colors and tolerance for travel. These qualities endear it to both the international plant trade and home growers. In five to seven years, a hybrid seedling like the one pictured to the right can form an impressive clump of pseudobulbs, the upper half to third of which retains evergreen foliage.

Flowers, each 3 to 4 inches in diameter, appear evenly spaced toward the outer reaches of graceful, reedlike stems (often 12 to 18 of them) 18 to 48 inches tall. One of the best qualities of this orchid is its ability to bloom from both old and new pseudobulbs. It's possible that Keiki Bell × Lady Charm will bloom on up to seven spikes at once from a plant established over a similar number of years.

TYPE: Epiphyte

GROWTH HABIT: Sympodial

ORIGINS: New Guinea, Australia

BLOOMING SEASON: Spring–summer, or at almost any time of year

LIGHT: High to medium; outdoors, in mostly sun but with some filtering of hottest rays through midday; indoors in a sunny window, or under multiple fluorescents or high-intensity light

TEMPERATURE: Intermediate to warm, ideally with days around 80°F, nights 10° cooler

HUMIDITY: High, and always in the presence of free air circulation

MOISTURE: Moist all year except somewhat less so in the fall; never so dry as to cause leaves or pseudobulbs to shrivel

GROWING MEDIUM: A, with perfect drainage

FERTILIZER: Weekly or every other week except for a brief rest in fall

PLANT SHOWN: Blooming in fall in a 4-inch pot

Dendrobium
hybrid

DENDROBIUM HYBRID

DENDROBIUM LINEALE × *DENDROBIUM* NEW HORIZON

Genus name is from the Greek dendros *(tree) and* bios *(life)*

This hybrid has the decidedly twisted upper petals of an antelope-type flower. Each of these curiously animated blooms is 2 to 3 inches in diameter and appears in the upper parts of a spike 2 to 4 feet tall. Flower colors range from golds to chestnut browns, with a touch of plum on the lip. Tolerance of a wide range of conditions, from humid to semi-arid, makes this an ideal confidence builder for the beginning orchid grower.

A hybrid *Dendrobium* of the antelope type grows all year round and doesn't require a chilling or drying period to initiate flowering. The spikes appear with enthusiasm on thrifty plants, most often in spring and summer but possibly at other seasons, especially if grown under a bank of fluorescents or a high-intensity light. As soon as the first buds open into flowers, the plant can be groomed and put on display for the duration of the season—for as much as three months of nonstop bloom.

The erect pseudobulbs of this hybrid, like its *D. lineale* parent, grow 2 to 4 feet tall and retain evergreen leaves 3 to 6 inches long, covering the upper two-thirds of growth. This makes an ideal launching pad to show off the arching inflorescence—10 to 30 inches long—bearing from 17 to as many as 50 fragrant flowers.

TYPE: Epiphyte

GROWTH HABIT: Sympodial

ORIGINS: Northern Australia, New Guinea

BLOOMING SEASON: Spring–summer, or at almost any time of year

LIGHT: High to medium; outdoors in mostly sun, but shaded at midday; indoors in a sunny window, or under multiple fluorescents or high-intensity light

TEMPERATURE: Intermediate to warm, ideally with days around 80°F, nights 10° cooler

HUMIDITY: High, and always in the presence of free air circulation

MOISTURE: Moist all year except somewhat less so in the fall; never so dry as to cause leaves or pseudobulbs to shrivel

GROWING MEDIUM: A, with perfect drainage

FERTILIZER: Weekly or every other week except for a brief rest in fall

PLANT SHOWN: Blooming in late spring in a 5-inch pot

Dendrobium
hybrid

DENDROBIUM PARISHII

Species named after its discoverer, Rev. C. Parish

This species is among the few flowers ever described as both rhubarb- and raspberry-scented. Long-lived flowers appear on short racemes of two or three (rarely, one), which grow from a node near the top of the plant. They are deep pink fading to white at the center, with a deep pink, purple-blotched lip. The oblong, lance-shaped leaves are 2 to 4 inches long, leathery or waxy green, sometimes growing into a second year but eventually deciduous, on canelike pseudobulbs that grow 6 to 24 inches high.

D. parishii is now known to occur naturally over a widespread region in Southeast Asia where average highest temperatures reach 87°F, lowest 46°F. Since these areas typically experience considerable cloud cover in the summer, it's well to position plants where they will have sufficient filtering of direct sun through midday to avoid leaf burn.

This species orchid will do well outdoors over much of North America throughout the summer as well as during the warmer parts of spring and fall. Flowering will not occur, however, unless there is a pronounced resting time of at least one if not two months in late fall or winter. In this stage, temperatures must be cooler but never freezing. Less water should be given, but extreme dryness should be avoided. If in doubt about watering, mist plants in early morning.

TYPE: Epiphyte

GROWTH HABIT: Sympodial

ORIGINS: Northeastern India, Burma, Thailand, Laos, Vietnam, southwestern China

BLOOMING SEASON: Early spring–summer

LIGHT: As high as the plant can tolerate short of burning the leaves; outdoors, in full sun except filtered at midday; indoors in or near a sunny window, or under multiple fluorescents or high-intensity lights

TEMPERATURE: Warm, ideally not below 60°F; cool (40°–50°F) while resting in late fall to early winter

HUMIDITY: Medium to high, with good air circulation

MOISTURE: Water freely during spring and summer; taper off in fall after new growths are established; expect leaves to gradually dry and drop

GROWING MEDIUM: A, with perfect drainage; in pots or baskets, or on tree-fern slabs

FERTILIZER: Weekly during spring and summer with 30-10-10; change to 15-30-15 in late summer and fall to encourage new canes to ripen and set buds

PLANT SHOWN: Blooming in early summer in a 5-inch pot

Dendrobium parishii

DORITAENOPSIS HYBRID

×*DORITAENOPSIS* ESCAPADE 'CANDY CANE' × *PHALAENOPSIS* BETTY HAUSERMANN

This hybrid was bred by Hausermann Orchids, the largest commercial grower of orchids in the United States. In appearance it closely resembles the parent *Phalaenopsis,* and so may also be called moth orchid.

Prized for its big, pale yellow flowers in winter, which last for months on end (often until the beginning of summer), ×*Doritaenopsis* is easily cultivated in the intermediate to warm temperatures commonly found in homes and offices. These orchids thrive in low to medium light, but a heavily shaded window or one facing north may not be bright enough. They grow well under fluorescent lights, until the height of a developing spike may necessitate a move to a window where there will be space for it to elongate normally.

Keep ×*Doritaenopsis* moist at all times. Water plants where they sit during the developmental period because changing the position of the pot will cause new growth, including flower spikes, to constantly twist in order to reorient toward the brightest light. Such a growth response isn't necessarily harmful, but it won't produce the most graceful specimen.

TYPE: Epiphyte

GROWTH HABIT: Monopodial

ORIGINS: Asia and Malaysia Archipelago

BLOOMING SEASON: Winter–spring, or at almost any season

LIGHT: Low to medium; outdoors with mostly shade, and preferably protected from hard rains and high winds; indoors under fluorescents or high-intensity light

TEMPERATURE: Warm to intermediate, with a winter low of 55°–65°F

HUMIDITY: High, but tolerant of less, with good air circulation

MOISTURE: Keep moist all year

GROWING MEDIUM: A or C (stressing seedling-grade bark)

FERTILIZER: Frequently during growing season, or three seasons out of four; very dilute applications of 30-10-10 may be used with four out of five waterings, with the fifth reserved for plain water to flush out any accumulated mineral salts

PLANT SHOWN: Blooming in spring in a 6-inch pot

Doritaenopsis
hybrid

DORITAENOPSIS HYBRID

✕*DORITAENOPSIS* FIRECRACKER 'MALIBU' HCC/AOS
(*DORITAENOPSIS* RED CORAL ✕ *DORITIS PULCHERRIMA*)

A hybrid genus created by crossing Doritis *and* Phalaenopsis

The hybrid 'Malibu' has received a High Commendation Certificate from the American Orchid Society and is worthy of inclusion in any collection where orchids of this type thrive. The unusually erect bloom spike of the plant shown indicates a plant grown without disturbance in ideal lighting conditions.

From its *Doritis pulcherrima* genes, ✕*Doritaenopsis* is often blessed with gorgeous cerise or striped coloration to its flowers. The striping or netting with a contrasting color gives the flowers an added dimension, as though they were being seen through a scrim. And the flowers—each up to 2 inches across—will last for months.

Because one of this hybrid's parents is *Doritis,* it will respond well to higher light than might its *Phalaenopsis* grandparent, exchanging plentiful blooms for a front-row seat at the window. These plants will also benefit from being potted in a finer mixture of medium A that includes seedling-grade bark (as in medium C).

Almost 1,500 species of ✕*Doritaenopsis* have been created since the inception of this lovely hybrid genus in 1923. These plants, like those of its *Phalaenopsis* forebear, are known as moth orchids.

TYPE: Epiphyte

GROWTH HABIT: Monopodial

ORIGINS: India, Malaysia, Indonesia

BLOOMING SEASON: Winter–spring, or at almost any time of year

LIGHT: Low to medium; outdoors, with mostly shade and preferably positioned where protected from hard rains and high winds; indoors under fluorescents or high-intensity light

TEMPERATURE: Warm to intermediate, with a winter nighttime low of 55°–65°F

HUMIDITY: High, but tolerant of less, with good air circulation

MOISTURE: Keep moist all year

GROWING MEDIUM: A or C (seedling-grade bark)

FERTILIZER: Apply frequently during growing season, or three seasons out of every four; dilute applications of 30-10-10 may be used with four out of five waterings, the fifth reserved for plain water to flush out any accumulated mineral salts

PLANT SHOWN: Blooming in spring in a 6-inch pot

Doritaenopsis
hybrid

DORITAENOPSIS HYBRID

✕*DORITAENOPSIS* HAUSERMANN'S
CHICAGO 'CANDY CLUSTER' AM/AOS ✕
✕*DORITAENOPSIS* HAUSERMANN'S CLASSIC 'VILLA PARK'

A hybrid genus created by crossing Doritis *and* Phalaenopsis

This extraordinary orchid has extravagantly large, well-formed flowers—up to 5 inches across—held with unusual grace by a 2- to 3-foot-tall wiry spike. The spike originates from relatively small, low-growing leaves up to 6 inches long and nearly half as wide.

The faint rose-pink candy striping with a contrasting dark rose-red lip makes these large flowers unusually noteworthy. Fortunately, this attribute is well grounded in a vigorous, easy-flowering plant that is as appropriate for a beginner as it is for an advanced collector.

It is not unusual for an ✕*Doritaenopsis* like the one shown, purchased in bloom, to adapt so well in the spot where it has been placed for display that it becomes something of a permanent fixture. A desk or table in bright light but shielded from direct sun can be ideal for both showing and growing these plants.

Hausermann's Chicago 'Candy Cluster' came from a cross of *Phalaenopsis* Carol Jean ✕ Michael Kaskas. The result of crossing it into the complex world of ✕*Doritaenopsis* Hausermann's Classic 'Villa Park' (Adam Carl ✕ Escape) is a bigger, more impressive flower than is typical of the candy-stripe orchids.

TYPE: Epiphyte

GROWTH HABIT: Monopodial

ORIGINS: India, Malaysia, Indonesia

BLOOMING SEASON: Winter–spring, or at almost any time of year

LIGHT: Low to medium; outdoors, with mostly shade and preferably positioned where protected from hard rains and high winds; indoors under fluorescents or high-intensity light

TEMPERATURE: Warm to intermediate, with a winter nighttime low of 55°–65°F

HUMIDITY: High, but tolerant of less, with good air circulation

MOISTURE: Keep moist all year

GROWING MEDIUM: A or C (seedling-grade bark)

FERTILIZER: Apply frequently during growing season, or three seasons out of every four; dilute applications of 30-10-10 may be used with four out of five waterings, the fifth reserved for plain water to flush out any accumulated mineral salts

PLANT SHOWN: Blooming in spring in a 6-inch pot

Doritaenopsis
hybrid

DORITAENOPSIS HYBRID

×*DORITAENOPSIS* HAUSERMANN'S CLASSIC 'SPIRIT'

The leaves and large, rounded, medium pink flowers with a ruby-red lip look remarkably like this orchid's *Phalaenopsis* forebears. The colors, however, suggest the *Doritis* side of the mix. The leaves of 'Spirit' are somewhat darker than the average moth orchid, with the upper surfaces veering to olive-green, the undersides burgundy-flushed. This coloration can indicate the need for—or at least a tolerance of—more light than similar plants with plain green foliage.

'Spirit' is prized for winter bloom, which can easily last in perfect condition for six to eight weeks. When the last flower drops, cutting the spike back to immediately above where the first bud originated (note visual evidence of such a cut on the plant in the photograph) can result in the formation of a secondary spike at that point. This can develop rapidly or may remain quiescent for a time, then seem to awaken suddenly and proceed to the hoped-for second flowering.

TYPE: Epiphyte

GROWTH HABIT: Monopodial

ORIGINS: A hybrid genus created in 1923

BLOOMING SEASON: Winter–spring, or at almost any season

LIGHT: Low to medium; outdoors with mostly shade, and preferably protected from hard rain and high winds; indoors under fluorescents or high-intensity light

TEMPERATURE: Warm to intermediate, with a winter low of 55°–65°F

HUMIDITY: Prefers high, but tolerant of less, with good air circulation

MOISTURE: Keep moist all year

GROWING MEDIUM: A or C (seedling-grade bark)

FERTILIZER: Apply frequently during the growing season, or three seasons out of four; very dilute applications of 30-10-10 may be used with four out of five waterings, with the fifth reserved for plain water to flush out any accumulated mineral salts

PLANT SHOWN: Blooming in spring in a 5-inch pot

Doritaenopsis
hybrid

DORITAENOPSIS HYBRID

×*DORITAENOPSIS* SEMINOLE 'ARMY TRAIL' × ×*DORITAENOPSIS* PURPLE SUNSET 'AFTERGLOW'

A hybrid genus created by crossing Doritis *and* Phalaenopsis

This complex hybrid, with its breathtakingly beautiful flower colors, represents a crossing of *Phalaenopsis* Seminole (Kenneth Benjamin × Peter Stromsland) with ×*Doritaenopsis* Purple Sunset 'Afterglow,' a yellow, dark purple, and peach blend.

Known categorically as a "yellow candy stripe," the individual flowers measure up to 3 inches across, and the spike may feature a few or many blooms at almost any length from 1 to 3 feet. The low-growing leaves—spanning up to 6 inches long by 3 inches wide—can take on a slight reddish sheen and be arrayed to suggest the shape and gracefulness of angel-wing begonias.

After an ×*Doritaenopsis* has grown into a 5- to 8-inch pot, flowering twice or even three times yearly is possible. After the first spike has flowered, cut it back approximately halfway, immediately above a node. Within three or four months a new flower stem will emerge and proceed to flower. When it finishes, the same cutting-back halfway can lead to yet a third flowering—from what began nearly a year earlier.

TYPE: Epiphyte

GROWTH HABIT: Monopodial

ORIGINS: India, Malaysia, Indonesia

BLOOMING SEASON: Winter–spring, or at almost any time of year

LIGHT: Low to medium; outdoors, with mostly shade and preferably positioned where protected from hard rains and high winds; indoors under fluorescents or high-intensity light

TEMPERATURE: Warm to intermediate, with a winter nighttime low of 55°–65°F

HUMIDITY: High, but tolerant of less, with good air circulation

MOISTURE: Keep moist all year

GROWING MEDIUM: A or C (seedling-grade bark)

FERTILIZER: Apply frequently during growing season, or three seasons out of every four; dilute applications of 30-10-10 may be used with four out of five waterings, the fifth reserved for plain water to flush out any accumulated mineral salts

PLANT SHOWN: Blooming in spring in a 6-inch pot

Doritaenopsis
hybrid

DORITIS HYBRID

DORITIS PULCHERRIMA 'ARLINGTON' × *DORITIS PULCHERRIMA*

Genus name is from the Greek dory *(spear), for the lip shape,*
and romantically for Doritis, one of the goddess Aphrodite's names

Doritis, a close ally of *Phalaenopsis,* has often been crossed with it to produce × *Doritaenopsis.* This orchid could easily go overlooked in a burgeoning world of ever bigger and splashier orchids. But a *Doritis* such as the pale- to medium-pink 'Arlington' is definitely worthy of a spot in any collection.

From basal leaves that grow up to 6 inches long by 3 inches wide, 'Arlington' sends up a flowering stalk 2 to 3 feet tall that branches and blooms successively almost indefinitely. This can be a superb display plant in the house, and is a good confidence builder for beginners.

The individual flowers may be hardly bigger than a silver dollar, yet by numbers, habit, and color, they can make quite a show. 'Arlington' has mauve-purple and purple flowers. In the cultivar *D. pulcherrima* 'Frank,' the flowers are uniformly vivid dark pink with white lines on the disc of the lip. *D. alba* × self flowers are white; *D. purpurea* are dark pink; and in the tetraploid *D. buyssoniana,* they are larger than the type in a rich lavender color.

TYPE: Epiphyte

GROWTH HABIT: Monopodial

ORIGINS: Man-made cultivar from an Indo-Malaysian species

BLOOMING SEASON: Summer

LIGHT: Medium; outdoors, bright, open shade, no direct sun; indoors in a partly sunny window or under high-intensity light

TEMPERATURE: Intermediate to warm, with low of 60°F and high of 80°F

HUMIDITY: High; 60% or more

MOISTURE: Water freely in warm weather, moderately at other times, but never allow to become extremely dry

GROWING MEDIUM: A, B or C (seedling-grade bark)

FERTILIZER: Spring and summer

PLANT SHOWN: Blooming in summer in a 6-inch pot

Doritis
hybrid

ENCYCLIA COCHLEATA

(SYN. *EPIDENDRUM COCHLEATUM*)

Genus name is from the Greek enkyklo *(to encircle),*
referring to the way in which the lip side lobes encircle the column

Considering the vast numbers of different orchids, it's worth noting that relatively few have a common name. This one has such an unusual flower it has two: "cockle orchid" and "clamshell orchid." Unlike most orchids, the shell-like lip (dark purple to nearly black, with a white spot toward the base and dark purple veining) of *Encyclia cochleata* is uppermost, while the narrow tepals (lime green) fall away like ribbons. The overall effect makes the flowers appear upside down, resembling an octopus.

The plant shown is young, perhaps in its first blossoming. Older specimens can have an inflorescence that continues to elongate for up to six months or more, reaching up to 18 inches tall and flowering successively over a delightfully long season, if not all year. *E. cochleata* is both easy to grow and to flower; moreover, the plants get on well with cattleyas and are often included in mixed collections of rainforest plants such as aroids, gesneriads, bromeliads, ferns, and palms.

This unique orchid also carries the distinction of being the first epiphytic orchid to have been flowered in England, in 1787—thirty-seven years before the first cattleya bloomed for horticulturist William Cattley in the autumn of 1824.

TYPE: Epiphyte

GROWTH HABIT: Sympodial

ORIGINS: Florida, the West Indies, Mexico south to Colombia and Venezuela

BLOOMING SEASON: Summer–fall

LIGHT: Medium to high; outdoors, in up to half a day of sun; indoors in a sunny window, or under fluorescent or high-intensity light

TEMPERATURE: Intermediate to warm, with a nighttime minimum of 60°F

HUMIDITY: Medium to high, always with free air circulation

MOISTURE: Moist in warm weather and until new growths have matured, then on the dry side (in cooler temperatures) until the beginning of the next active growing season

GROWING MEDIUM: A

FERTILIZER: Spring–summer

PLANT SHOWN: Blooming in late spring in a 3-inch pot

Encyclia
cochleata

ENCYCLIA CORDIGERA

(SYN. *EPIDENDRUM ATROPURPUREUM*)

Genus name is from the Greek enkyklo *(to encircle),*
referring to the way in which the lip side lobes encircle the column

At first glance, the orchid novice is almost certain to confuse this lovely flower with a *Cattleya*. In fact this assessment, by strict botanical observation, would not be so far-fetched since the presence of pseudobulbs makes it appear more like a *Cattleya* than an *Epidendrum*. The earliest records in 1815 use the name *Cymbidium cordigerum,* which later gave way to *Epidendrum*. R. Dressler placed the species in *Encyclia* in 1964, but the plant is still traded and used in hybridizing as *Epidendrum atropurpureum*.

This medium-size plant has a grassy appearance and when in flower makes a nearly perfect orchid for display in the home. Anywhere from three to fifteen long-lasting, fragrant flowers appear on each long spray that rises from the top of the short, oval pseudobulbs. The mahogany or purplish-brown and green tepals are wide-spreading and thus emphasize the showy dark-crimson-striped white lip.

In climates where it can be grown outdoors most or all of the year, or kept in a greenhouse during cold weather, *Encyclia cordigera* is perhaps best shown off when mounted on bark. This assures the plant free air circulation, and provided it's moistened consistently, never dries it to the point of shriveling the pseudobulbs. Given such care, a breathtaking specimen can develop with many leads pointing upward and a crown of flowers.

TYPE: Epiphyte

GROWTH HABIT: Sympodial

ORIGINS: Mexico, Central America, Colombia, Venezuela

BLOOMING SEASON: Spring

LIGHT: Medium to high; outdoors, in up to half a day of sun; indoors in a sunny window, or under fluorescents or high-intensity light

TEMPERATURE: Intermediate to warm, with a nighttime minimum of 60°F

HUMIDITY: Medium to high, always with free air circulation

MOISTURE: Moist in warm weather and until new growths have matured, then on the dry side (in cooler temperatures) until the beginning of the next active growing season

GROWING MEDIUM: A, or on a bark mount

FERTILIZER: Spring–summer

PLANT SHOWN: Blooming in spring in a 5-inch pot

*Encyclia
cordigera*

ENCYCLIA HYBRID

ENCYCLIA TAMPENSIS × 'PAGODA'
(SYN. *EPIDENDRUM TAMPENSE*)

Genus name is from the Greek enkyklo *(to encircle),*
referring to the way in which the lip side lobes encircle the column

This is a larger, showier cultivar of a much-loved orchid native to Florida and the Bahamas known officially as *Encyclia tampensis,* but more commonly as *Epidendrum tampense.* Unsophisticated dealers once sold these orchids collected from the wild as "butterfly orchids," a common name more correctly applied to *Psychopsis.* Even in the smaller-flowered species *Encyclia tampensis,* novices quickly recognize the similarity with the blossoms of *Cattleya,* which technically are no different except for their much larger size.

The small flowers of *E. tampensis* are lightly fragrant—as are the larger, more vividly colored flowers of the hybrid shown here. The flowers have greenish tepals and a purplish lip. This species, along with its progeny, may bloom at almost any time, particularly in spring and summer, and with sufficient numbers and longevity to make them popular with collectors.

This orchid is native to North America but has all but disappeared from the wild, owing to destruction of habitat. An additional satisfaction that comes from growing *E. tampensis* and its offspring has to do with keeping alive something precious to our heritage that might otherwise become extinct.

TYPE: Epiphyte

GROWTH HABIT: Sympodial

ORIGINS: Species *E. tampensis* native to Florida and the Bahamas

BLOOMING SEASON: Spring–summer

LIGHT: Medium to high; outdoors, in up to half a day of sun; indoors in a sunny window, or under fluorescent or high-intensity light

TEMPERATURE: Intermediate to warm, with a nighttime minimum of 60°F

HUMIDITY: Medium to high, always with free air circulation

MOISTURE: Moist in warm weather and until new growths have matured, then on the dry side (in cooler temperatures) until the beginning of the next active growing season

GROWING MEDIUM: A, or mounted on bark

FERTILIZER: Spring and summer

PLANT SHOWN: Blooming in spring in a 3-inch pot

Encyclia
hybrid

ENCYCLIA MARIAE

(SYN. *EPIDENDRUM MARIAE*)

Genus name is from the Greek enkyklo *(to encircle),*
referring to the way in which the lip side lobes encircle the column

The stunning flower display of this orchid is an altogether cooling sight in summer or early fall, the usual flowering season for *Encyclia mariae*. The tepals are lime- to olive-green and the large, pristinely white lip has green veins in the throat. The plant sends out 4-inch leaves from 2-inch pseudobulbs, above which the green and white flowers appear on a stem about 8 inches tall. Unless staked in an upright position, the weight of these gorgeous blooms will tend to bring the spike down to a more pendent position.

This orchid is particularly sensitive to high temperatures. Unless air-conditioning is available in a greenhouse or in suitably bright home conditions, it is not recommended where summers mean protracted high temperatures above 80°F. It does best in a relatively cool spot, but can be helped in tolerating short periods of hot weather if provided with some extra shade and free air circulation. Since flowering occurs in summer, the simple solution in most of North America for hot weather is to display the plant where there is air-conditioning, then return it to the growing area after the worst heat is over.

TYPE: Epiphyte

GROWTH HABIT: Sympodial

ORIGINS: Mexico

BLOOMING SEASON: Summer–fall

LIGHT: Medium to high; outdoors, in up to half a day of sun; indoors in a sunny window, or under fluorescent or high-intensity light

TEMPERATURE: Intermediate, with a nighttime minimum of 60°F

HUMIDITY: Medium to high, always with good air circulation

MOISTURE: Moist in warm weather and until new growths have matured, then on the dry side (in cooler temperatures) until the beginning of the next active growing season

GROWING MEDIUM: A

FERTILIZER: Spring and summer

PLANT SHOWN: Blooming in early summer in a 5-inch pot

*Encyclia
mariae*

GOMESA RECURVA

(SYN. *RODRIGUEZIA RECURVA; ODONTOGLOSSUM RECURVUM*)

Genus named for Dr. Bernadino Antonio Gomes,
a Portuguese naval physician and botanist

This is not a flashy orchid, but collectors seek it out for several reasons: the small flowers are primarily pale lime- or yellowish-green, which is unusual; they give off a light, sweet fragrance; and the flowers appear in generous numbers on a downward-bound inflorescence. Their usual flowering season of fall and winter makes them especially welcome to any orchid collection, and it's during this time that the plants can take more light. Their bloom time makes them appropriate candidates for hanging pots or placement on the upper shelves in a window or greenhouse.

Gomesa recurva is one of about twenty species in the genus, and all are native to Brazil. The strongly recurving lip gives the species its name, and the arrangement of the tepals might well suggest a protective human figure. It was first flowered in a greenhouse at the Chelsea Botanic Garden in London, and described in 1815.

G. crispa is of similar habit, also providing fragrant flowers in a pendent, arching inflorescence. Its floral parts are mostly waved at the edges (hence, *crispa*) and the color can vary from yellow to lime, olive, or sea-green with yellow edging. In *G. planifolia* the flowers are slightly smaller than in the other two species described; they are of similar coloration but are more intensely fragrant.

TYPE: Epiphyte or lithophyte

GROWTH HABIT: Sympodial

ORIGINS: Brazil

BLOOMING SEASON: Fall–winter

LIGHT: Medium; outdoors, in half sun to partial shade; indoors in a partly sunny window, or under fluorescent or high-intensity light; increase light in the season following completion of new growth

TEMPERATURE: Intermediate, with a nighttime minimum of 60°F

HUMIDITY: Medium to high, with good air movement

MOISTURE: Water freely when in active growth, less following completion of new growth, but take care that the pseudobulbs remain firm

GROWING MEDIUM: A

FERTILIZER: Spring and summer

PLANT SHOWN: Blooming in summer in a 6-inch pot

Gomesa
recurva

KAGAWARA HYBRID

×*KAGAWARA* RED LAVA 'ORANGE GLOW'
(*RENANTHERA IMSCHOOTIANA* ×
×*ASCOCENDA* MEDA ARNOLD)

A hybrid genus combining Renanthera *and* Ascocenda (Ascocentrum × Vanda)

Not introduced until after the first hybrid of *Renanthera* was registered in 1931 (×*Renanthopsis* Premier [*Renanthera imschootiana* × *Phalaenopsis sanderiana*]), the hybrid genus ×*Kagawara* has rapidly risen to prominence among savvy collectors. The compact, outwardly attractive plants are typically crowned by one or more erect inflorescences of 2- to 3-inch flowers of vivid reds, oranges, and other flame colors. Many amateurs succeed in getting bloom twice yearly, and the flowers last perfectly on the plants for up to six weeks.

The parent *Renanthera imschootiana* originates from northeastern India and Burma. Its summer-blooming pale orange or yellow flowers, 1 to 1½ inches across, are spotted with deep red. The long-stemmed, liana-like plants have short, rigid leaves 2 to 5 inches long.

The other parent, ×*Ascocenda,* is a fortuitous hybrid combination of both its parents' most admirable features—the relatively small, compact plant size typical of *Ascocentrum* combined with the large flowers of the *Vanda.* All these traits are carried into ×*Kagawara,* thus putting it on the short list of the most discerning collectors.

TYPE: Epiphyte

GROWTH HABIT: Monopodial

ORIGIN: Southeast Asia, Himalayas to Malaysia

BLOOMING SEASON: Spring–summer, or at almost any time of year

LIGHT: Medium to high; outdoors, with some diffusion of hot, direct sun through midday to avoid leaf scorch; indoors in a sunny window, or under multiple fluorescents or high-intensity light

TEMPERATURE: Intermediate, with a winter minimum of 60°F; best to avoid summer temperatures above 80°F

HUMIDITY: Medium to high, always with good air circulation

MOISTURE: Water freely, except somewhat less during the coolest, shortest days of the year

GROWING MEDIUM: A

FERTILIZER: Lightly, frequently, regularly in spring and summer

PLANT SHOWN: Blooming in early summer in a 7-inch pot

Kagawara
hybrid

LAELIA HYBRID

LAELIA PURPURATA 'CINDAROSA'

Genus named after one of the Vestal Virgins

The plant pictured is a mericlone of a selected *Laelia purpurata* 'Cindarosa,' and is admired for its generosity of gorgeous blooms—five at once is not unusual for a relatively young plant. Spanning up to 6 inches across, the individual flowers have snowy white, translucent petals and sepals that showcase a vibrantly purple lip; they also give off a seductive perfume.

Hybrids of *L. purpurata,* among them 'Cindarosa,' often bloom in the spring and again in late summer or fall. Although it wouldn't be sound cultural practice to grow this beauty with the surface roots and growing medium covered with moss, a carpeting of live sheet moss or woods moss at the time of bloom creates a beautiful effect and helps call attention to the plant's sculptural form.

The cultural needs of this orchid are fairly easy to provide in both temperate and tropical climates where the plants can be readily accommodated outdoors in warm, frost-free weather and brought to almost any warm, bright, sunny location during other seasons. *Laelia* plants that are given ample light, moisture, and nutrients outdoors for a season can also be readily managed at other times in a greenhouse or bay window, or under artificial light.

TYPE: Epiphyte or lithophyte

GROWTH HABIT: Sympodial

ORIGINS: Southern Brazil

BLOOMING SEASON: March–November

LIGHT: Medium to high; outdoors, provide enough shade through midday to prevent leaf scorch; indoors in a sunny window, or under multiple fluorescents or high-intensity light

TEMPERATURE: Intermediate to warm, with a minimum of 55°–62°F on winter nights

HUMIDITY: Moderate to high, always in the presence of good air circulation

MOISTURE: Water freely while in active growth during spring and summer, somewhat less in fall and winter, but never allow to become dry enough to shrivel the leaves or pseudobulbs

GROWING MEDIUM: A

FERTILIZER: Lightly, frequently, regularly in spring and summer, less in fall, little or none in winter

PLANT SHOWN: Blooming in spring in a 6-inch pot

Laelia
hybrid

LAELIA HYBRID

LAELIA PURPURATA VAR. ACO ERNESTO × *LAELIA PURPURATA* VAR. *CARNEA*

Genus named after one of the Vestal Virgins

The result of this unusual crossing is one of the finest and largest flowers in its class. Because of its dramatic blooms, *Laelia purpurata* has been widely used in hybridization and often figures in the parentage of any *Laelia* characterized as having large, unusually showy flowers that are primarily white with a vibrant pink to rose lip.

An ordinarily spring-blooming *Laelia* may, in practice, erupt in unsurpassed bloom at almost any time from spring until fall. These are superb display plants, with individual flowers lasting for three to four weeks.

The type species, *L. purpurata* (the national flower of Brazil), bears two to five flowers that are 8 inches in diameter on each 8- to 12-inch inflorescence. The fragrant flowers vary in color, but those on the hybrid shown are white with the inside of the lip and throat striped with deep pink. The dark green, leathery leaves are oblong, to 8 inches long or more, and to almost 2 inches across.

TYPE: Epiphyte or lithophyte

GROWTH HABIT: Sympodial

ORIGINS: Southern Brazil

BLOOMING SEASON: March–November

LIGHT: Medium to high; outdoors, provide enough shade through midday to prevent leaf scorch; indoors in a sunny window, under multiple fluorescents or high-intensity light

TEMPERATURE: Intermediate to warm, with a minimum of 55°–62°F on winter nights

HUMIDITY: Moderate to high, always in the presence of good air circulation

MOISTURE: Water freely while in active growth during spring and summer, somewhat less in fall and winter, but never allow to become dry enough to shrivel the leaves or pseudobulbs

GROWING MEDIUM: A

FERTILIZER: Lightly, frequently, regularly in spring and summer, less in fall, little or none in winter

PLANT SHOWN: Blooming in spring in a 5-inch pot

Laelia
hybrid

LAELIOCATTLEYA HYBRID

×*LAELIOCATTLEYA* ACKER'S SPOTLIGHT 'PINK LADY'
(*CATTLEYA ACLANDIAE* × ACKER'S MADISON)

A hybrid genus created by crossing Laelia *and* Cattleya

The vivid pink-lavender flowers of this clone give off a pronounced sweet fragrance. They appear in summer or fall and are exceptionally well suited to display indoors. A waxy substance on the flowers allows them to last well for up to a week when cut, or up to a month or more on the plant.

Cattleya aclandiae, one of the parents of *Laeliocattleya* 'Pink Lady,' forms a dwarf, compact plant with medium-size, fragrant flowers that are strikingly colored and patterned. The sepals and petals are pinkish tan with purple-brown leopard-like spotting or even cross-banding. The lip is a bright amethyst-purple or cerise-pink.

This orchid was discovered in Brazil in the fall of 1839 and flowered the next year in England. In their natural setting, the plants grow in trees under relatively dry conditions but near the coast, where the air is sufficiently moist to sustain them during periods of low or no rainfall.

TYPE: Epiphyte

GROWTH HABIT: Sympodial

ORIGINS: Tropical Central and South America

BLOOMING SEASON: Summer–fall

LIGHT: Medium to high; outdoors, provide enough filtering shade to prevent leaf scorch; indoors in a sunny window, or under multiple fluorescents or high-intensity light

TEMPERATURE: Intermediate, with a minimum of 55°–60°F on winter nights

HUMIDITY: Medium to high, with good air circulation

MOISTURE: Water generously during spring and summer, with a bit of drying between waterings; less in fall and winter, but never allow to become dry enough to shrivel the pseudobulbs

GROWING MEDIUM: A

FERTILIZER: Regularly in spring and summer, less in fall and winter

PLANT SHOWN: Blooming in summer in a 7-inch pot

Laeliocattleya
hybrid

LAELIOCATTLEYA HYBRID

✕*LAELIOCATTLEYA* DOROTHY FIENE 'SPRING FEVER'
(✕*LAELIOCATTLEYA* TIME LIFE ✕ ARLENE MARIE)

'Spring Fever' is an appropriate cultivar name for this orchid because it can be counted on to bloom gloriously each spring. The flowers are truly a visual and sensual wonder, growing 6 to 8 inches across with a large, ruffled lip of velvety amethyst-purple that sets off a glowing golden marking within.

✕*Laeliocattleya* orchids bear large blossoms that last about a month on strong stems. They enjoy medium light and medium temperatures; a medium-coarse mix of bark and perlite is perfect for potting. Water and fertilize these plants regularly, but allow them to dry out a bit between waterings; fertilizer can be cut down when their growth period is over.

Although the hybrid genus ✕*Laeliocattleya* occurs naturally, it was engineered in 1863, becoming the first man-made intergeneric orchid genus. Gardeners more attuned to the simple pleasures of growing beautiful orchids may not even notice the difference between what the botanist recognizes as an ✕*Laeliocattleya* and a pure *Cattleya*.

TYPE: Epiphyte or lithophyte
GROWTH HABIT: Sympodial
ORIGINS: Tropical America
BLOOMING SEASON: Spring
LIGHT: Medium to bright; outdoors, with only enough shading through midday to prevent leaf scorch; indoors in a sunny window, or under multiple fluorescents or high-intensity light
TEMPERATURE: Intermediate, with a winter low of 55°–60°F
HUMIDITY: Medium to high, always in the presence of freely circulating fresh air

MOISTURE: Water freely, let dry a bit, then water again; maintain somewhat less moisture in fall and winter, but never allow to become so dry as to shrivel the leaves or pseudobulbs; in times of cold, cloudy weather, it may be better to mist the plants and pseudobulbs rather than to apply water at the roots
GROWING MEDIUM: A
FERTILIZER: Light, frequently, regularly when plants are growing, usually during spring and summer
PLANT SHOWN: Blooming in spring in a 6-inch pot

Laeliocattleya
hybrid

LAELIOCATTLEYA HYBRID

×*LAELIOCATTLEYA* GOLD DIGGER 'BUTTERCUP'
(RED GOLD × *CATTLEYA* WARPAINT)

A naturally occurring and man-made hybrid genus from crossing Cattleya *and* Laelia

This orchid caused a stir beginning with its introduction in 1974—a propitious timing for several reasons. When 'Buttercup' was first introduced, there was widespread interest but few options in miniature plants that could be cultivated indoors. Also, the tissue culturing of superior plants had left the purely scientific world and entered the nursery business. And the number of amateur orchid collectors was on the rise.

'Buttercup' is no shrinking violet of a miniature plant, merely smaller than most of the cattleyas and laelias known at the time of its introduction. In terms of mass appeal, it's arguably the perfect size, habit, and flower color; it blooms at any time from midwinter through spring; plus it's floriferous and easy to flower, with long-lasting blooms.

Furthermore, meristemming has made the price ideal for the average beginning collector. Starter plants usually cost around $10, and splendid specimens sporting dozens of flowers are around $50.

TYPE: Epiphyte or lithophyte

GROWTH HABIT: Sympodial

ORIGINS: Tropical America

BLOOMING SEASON: Winter–spring

LIGHT: Medium to bright; outdoors, with only enough shading through midday to prevent outright leaf scorch; indoors in a sunny window, or under multiple fluorescents or high-intensity light

TEMPERATURE: Intermediate, with a winter low of 55°–60°F

HUMIDITY: Medium to high, always in the presence of freely circulating fresh air

MOISTURE: Water freely, let dry a bit, then water again; maintain somewhat less moist in fall and winter, but never so dry as to shrivel the leaves or pseudobulbs; in times of cold, cloudy weather, it may be better to mist the plants and pseudobulbs rather than to apply water at the roots.

GROWING MEDIUM: A

FERTILIZER: Lightly, frequently, regularly during active growth, usually in spring and summer

PLANT SHOWN: Blooming in spring in a 6-inch pot

Laeliocattleya
hybrid

LAELIOCATTLEYA HYBRID

×*LAELIOCATTLEYA* MARY ELIZABETH BOHN
'ROYAL FLARE' AM/AOS
(BLUE BOY × *CATTLEYA BOWRINGIANA*)

A naturally occurring and man-made hybrid genus created by crossing Cattleya *and* Laelia

'Royal Flare' is often described a "splash blue," for the seemingly splashed darker color over the face of the flower, particularly the petals. Color-sensitive eyes will immediately pick this plant out of a crowd of orchids as being blue (although not as clearly blue as some vandas or notably blue garden flowers).

The inflorescences, standing to nearly 2 feet high atop the unifoliate pseudobulbs, each contain seven perfectly spaced flowers, 4 to 5 inches across. The blooms give off a powdery, sweet smell.

Cattleya bowringia, the grandparent species, has narrow, oblong leaves, 6 to 8 inches long, that are leathery and dark green. The pretty flowers, purple with a lighter shade toward the base of the lip and a darker shade toward the edge of the lip, appear in inflorescences of 5 to 15, and rarely to 30 or more. White blotches line each blossom's throat.

TYPE: Epiphyte or lithophyte

GROWTH HABIT: Sympodial

ORIGINS: Tropical America

BLOOMING SEASON: Summer–fall

LIGHT: Medium to bright; outdoors, with only enough shading through midday to prevent outright leaf scorch; indoors in a sunny window, or under multiple fluorescents or high-intensity light

TEMPERATURE: Intermediate, with a winter low of 55°–60°F

HUMIDITY: Medium to high, always in the presence of freely circulating fresh air

MOISTURE: Water freely, let dry a bit, then water again; maintain somewhat less moist in fall and winter, but never so dry as to shrivel the leaves or pseudobulbs; in times of cold, cloudy weather, it may be better to mist the plants and pseudobulbs rather than to apply water at the roots.

GROWING MEDIUM: A

FERTILIZER: Lightly, frequently, regularly during active growth, usually in spring and summer

PLANT SHOWN: Blooming in fall in a 10-inch pot

Laeliocattleya
hybrid

LAELIOCATTLEYA HYBRID

×*LAELIOCATTLEYA* MEMORIA RAFAEL CITRON 'RUSTY'

A naturally occurring and man-made hybrid genus created by crossing Cattleya *and* Laelia

G reen flowers that gradually open over a period of days or weeks and turn a glowing rust color are this orchid's strongest attraction, along with a surprising lemon-verbena perfume. Appropriately named 'Rusty,' this orchid is the result of a cross of *Cattleya* Adula and ×*Laeliocattleya* Golden Joy.

For the person who is fond of the so-called art shades, or blended colors, 'Rusty' is a treasure. Although its coloring changes, there is always the subtlety associated with the art shades, a term used to describe almost any blended color that cannot be described in the more usual terms of red, pink, or rose, for example.

The "Memoria" (abbreviated as "Mem." on pot labels and in catalogs) indicates that the orchid is named in memory of Rafael Citron.

'Rusty' is considered fall-blooming. From year to year and collection to collection, it has been known to flower in late summer or not until early winter. It has four or five 4-inch flowers that appear above recently matured bifoliate growths, 15 to 18 inches tall.

TYPE: Epiphyte, lithophyte

GROWTH HABIT: Sympodial

ORIGINS: Tropical America

BLOOMING SEASON: Fall–winter

LIGHT: Medium to bright; outdoors, with only enough shading through midday to prevent leaf scorch; indoors in a sunny window, or under multiple fluorescents or high-intensity light

TEMPERATURE: Intermediate, with a winter nighttime low of 55°–60°F

HUMIDITY: Medium to high, always in the presence of freely circulating air

MOISTURE: Water freely, let dry a bit, then water again; water somewhat less in fall and winter, but never allow to become so dry as to shrivel the leaves or pseudobulbs; in times of cold, cloudy weather, it may be better practice to mist the plants and pseudobulbs rather than water the roots directly

GROWING MEDIUM: A

FERTILIZER: Lightly, frequently, regularly during active growth

PLANT SHOWN: Blooming in fall in a 6-inch pot

Laeliocattleya
hybrid

LAELIOCATTLEYA HYBRID

✕*LAELIOCATTLEYA* MINI PURPLE 'TAMAMI' BM/JOGA

A naturally occurring and man-made hybrid genus created by crossing Cattleya *and* Laelia

Mini Purple resulted from a cross between *Laelia pumila* and *Cattleya walkeriana,* and was registered in 1991. Both species are basically small plants with large flowers. 'Tamami' has received the Brown Medal from the Japanese Orchid Growers Association and stands as the quintessential miniature orchid in its class.

Mini Purple's plant is unifoliate above slender, grooved pseudobulbs, 1 to 2 inches tall and ½ inch in diameter. The leaves are 3 to 4 inches long and ¾ inch wide; flowers are 2 to 3 inches across, perfectly formed, and vividly colored.

Without question, this is one of the great orchids for the indoor gardener. It does, however, need consistently high humidity, which can be provided by anyone who is genuinely committed to growing such plants in the indoor environment. A word of caution: if your humidity is on the low side, watering the plant more will not make up for the lack of moisture in the air—it will only lead to root rot.

TYPE: Epiphyte or lithophyte

GROWTH HABIT: Sympodial

ORIGINS: Tropical America

BLOOMING SEASON: Fall–winter

LIGHT: Medium to bright; outdoors, with only enough shading through midday to prevent outright leaf scorch; indoors in a sunny window, or under multiple fluorescents or high-intensity light

TEMPERATURE: Intermediate, with a winter low of 55°–60°F

HUMIDITY: Preferably high, always in the presence of freely circulating fresh air

MOISTURE: Water freely, let dry a bit, then water again; maintain somewhat less moist in fall and winter, but never so dry as to shrivel the leaves or pseudobulbs; in times of cold, cloudy weather, it may be better to mist the plants and pseudobulbs rather than to apply water at the roots

GROWING MEDIUM: A

FERTILIZER: Lightly, frequently, regularly during active growth, usually in spring and summer

PLANT SHOWN: Blooming in fall in a 3-inch pot

Laeliocattleya
hybrid

LEPTOTES BICOLOR

From the Greek, leptotes *(delicateness), referring to the delicate
leaves of many species in the genus*

This utterly charming miniature has many fine qualities. The terete leaves, 4 to 5 inches tall, seem more leathery thick than delicate. The 2-inch flowers have narrow tepals that curve forward almost in a protective gesture around the bright magenta lip, which has a dark purple column. The flowers give off a light, sweet scent and are likely to appear in late winter or early spring—their timing makes them most welcome in a window or light garden.

Orchid plants this small need careful watering to prevent both lingering wetness and dryness. For this reason, they are better suited to shallow pots or bark mounts. They need less moisture in fall and winter, but never so little that their leaves shrivel. Moist air that circulates freely is a boon in all circumstances—indoors or out, in sun or under electric lights.

Leptotes bicolor was discovered in the Organ Mountains near Rio de Janeiro, Brazil, and first described by the British botanist John Lindley in 1833. The seed capsule, which contains vanillin, is used for flavoring in Brazil.

The even smaller, also fragrant *L. unicolor* (white-pink to pale rose-lilac) was found on the branches of trees growing along the banks of the River Dourado near Alfenas, Brazil, around 1877.

TYPE: Epiphyte

GROWTH HABIT: Sympodial

ORIGINS: Eastern Brazil, Paraguay

BLOOMING SEASON: Winter–summer

LIGHT: Medium; outdoors, in half sun to partial shade; indoors in a partly sunny window, or under fluorescent or high-intensity light

TEMPERATURE: Intermediate to warm, with a nighttime minimum of 60°F

HUMIDITY: Medium to light, with good air movement

MOISTURE: Nicely moist during spring and summer; less so in the season after flowering, but not so dry as to shrivel the leaves or rhizomes

GROWING MEDIUM: A, or on a bark mount

FERTILIZER: spring and summer

PLANT SHOWN: Blooming in spring in a 3-inch pot

*Leptotes
bicolor*

LYCASTE LOCUSTA

Genus named for a daughter of King Priam of Troy

O f all the green flower possibilities, this one is arguably the most distinctive. Sea green tepals—to 3 inches across or more— have a sideways flare that reveals a broader, darker green lip, which is fringed and white-margined. The flowers appear singly atop a reedlike stem well above the graceful, lightly pleated foliage. From top to bottom, this orchid provides a singular display.

The genus *Lycaste* was first described by John Lindley in 1843 and subsequently, numerous species were attributed to *Maxillaria*—a chief difference being the pleated leaves of the true lycastes, of which there are about 45 species.

Lycaste locusta and the similar *L. longipetala* (yellow-green with a tinge of brown, and the lip red-brown or violet-purple) produce individual flowers that last quite a long time. In fact, a healthy, mature specimen can bloom for several months. The spikes emerge from the base of the pseudobulbs as new leaves make their appearance.

L. locusta, L. longipetala, and other species hailing from cooler, mountainous regions generally get along well with cymbidiums. The chief difference is that they are deciduous, while cymbidiums are evergreen. The lycastes should thus be kept quite dry in winter; increase watering as the days grow longer and the gradually increasing temperatures of spring awaken the resting pseudobulbs. New root growth will boost fresh, young leaves and, hopefully, the spikes that produce blooms by summer.

TYPE: Epiphyte, lithophyte, terrestrial

GROWTH HABIT: Sympodial

ORIGINS: Peru

BLOOMING SEASON: Spring–summer

LIGHT: Medium; outdoors, in half sun to part shade; indoors in a partly sunny window, or under fluorescents or high-intensity light

TEMPERATURE: Intermediate to cool, with a low of 50°F and never warmer than 80°F

HUMIDITY: Medium

MOISTURE: Water freely during active growth, then decrease gradually until the leaves die down; water sparingly through a cool, dry resting period; when new shoots appear, gradually increase watering

GROWING MEDIUM: B

FERTILIZER: Spring and summer

PLANT SHOWN: Blooming in late spring in a 6-inch pot

*Lycaste
locusta*

LYCASTE MITCHELLII

Genus named for a daughter of King Priam of Troy

The yellow-flowered lycastes are easily managed if they can be kept sufficiently cool in summer and dry in winter. Unless required for propagation purposes, it's better not to divide and repot these orchids. Instead, keep them in the same pot and they will grow numerous, long-lasting flowers that appear at the base of the pseudobulbs. Resist the urge to touch the flowers, however, as this will cause bruising and premature aging.

The plant pictured is labeled *Lycaste mitchellii,* and while this name has not been found in any reference, Gene Hausermann, owner of Hausermann Orchids, says he remembers it blooming in his family's collection when he was a boy. The flowers' bright yellow/yellow-orange coloring and cinnamon scent suggest *L. aromatica,* which grows both epiphytically and lithophytically in Mexico, Guatemala, and Nicaragua. The addition of a dark red blotch and dimple at the base of the lip, however, suggests another species, *L. cruenta* (from Mexico, Guatemala, and El Salvador), which is also characterized as being "rather variable" and appearing in "several distinct forms."

TYPE: Epiphyte, lithophyte

GROWTH HABIT: Sympodial

ORIGINS: Tropical America

BLOOMING SEASON: Spring

LIGHT: Medium; outdoors, with enough filtering of direct sun through midday to prevent leaf scorch; indoors in a partly sunny window, or under fluorescents or high-intensity light

TEMPERATURE: Intermediate to cool, with a low of 50°F and never warmer than 80°F

HUMIDITY: Medium to high, and always with good air movement

MOISTURE: Water freely during active growth, then taper off gradually until the leaves die down; water sparingly through a cool, dry resting period; during this time it may be preferable to mist the pseudobulbs rather than apply water to the roots; when new shoots appear, gradually increase watering

GROWING MEDIUM: A or C

FERTILIZER: Lightly, frequently in spring and summer

PLANT SHOWN: Blooming in late spring in a 4-inch pot

*Lycaste
mitchellii*

MASDEVALLIA INFRACTA

(SYNS. *MASDEVALLIA LONGICAUDATA*, *MASDEVALLIA ALBIDA*)

Genus named for Dr. José Masdeval, eighteenth-century Spanish physician and botanist

Some will view this little orchid as a jewel; others will dismiss it immediately. The flower form is remarkably different from other orchids, and the coloration is complex and varied. The outside of the flower is purplish pink to dull red with a yellow flush; inside, it is purple to wine red. There are also faintly yellow tails, white petals, a red-brown spotted lip tip, and a yellow-white perianth-tube. So nuanced are the colors that a magnifying glass will help in the appreciation of these otherworldly flowers.

The leaves are 5 to 6 inches long, and the bell-shaped, pendant flowers rise on slender stalks to about twice that height. Each lasts for up to a month.

Minimum temperatures for this orchid are around 50°F, but they are not as critical as the maximum temperature, which should never exceed 80°F. A fluorescent-light garden in a room that can be temperature-controlled through air-conditioning is often the way to succeed with masdevallias, even in climates with torrid summers.

Although individual plants are small, the genus *Masdevallia* is quite large, containing some 340 species found from Mexico through tropical South America. They become increasingly diverse in the Andes, from Peru to Venezuela.

TYPE: Epiphyte

GROWTH HABIT: Sympodial

ORIGINS: Mountainous forests of Brazil and Peru

BLOOMING SEASON: Spring–summer

LIGHT: Low to medium; outdoors, in shade; indoors in a window with shade, or under fluorescents

TEMPERATURE: Intermediate to cool, with a low of 50°F and never above 80°F

HUMIDITY: High, with good air circulation

MOISTURE: Keep moist all year, ideally with clean rainwater, taking care to avoid extremes of wet and dry

GROWING MEDIUM: A

FERTILIZER: Sparingly, and not at all during periods of stress (such as during warm temperatures)

PLANT SHOWN: Blooming in summer in a 4-inch pot

*Masdevallia
infracta*

MASDEVALLIA MARGUERITE

M. INFRACTA × *M. VEITCHIANA*

Genus named for Dr. José Masdeval, eighteenth-century Spanish physician and botanist

The combination of bright, warm red color with yellow markings makes this orchid stand out, especially in the relatively low light where masdevallias grow and bloom. A vigorous hybrid, it will quickly fill a small pot with growths that send up a profusion of flowers, each lasting about a month.

Since flowering tends to occur between fall and spring, these plants are ideal cold-weather companions for indoor gardeners. Their primary needs are coolness, lots of moisture, and low light.

About 350 species of *Masdevallia* grow from Mexico to Brazil, but most are found in the Andes of Colombia, Ecuador, and Peru. They are essentially epiphytes, although some are found growing as lithophytes and terrestrials. Current breeding has vastly increased interest in the genus and produced larger, showier flowers.

The parent *M. infracta* (see pages 116–117) is known for its unique flowers, not typical of orchids. The larger parent, *M. veitchiana,* comes from southeastern Peru near Machu Picchu. It produces single scarlet flowers with short-tailed sepals on tall stems above upright leaves, which can grow to 10 inches long.

TYPE: Epiphyte

GROWTH HABIT: Sympodial

ORIGINS: Mountainous forests of Brazil and Peru

BLOOMING SEASON: Spring–summer

LIGHT: Low to medium; outdoors, in shade; indoors in a window with shade, or under fluorescents

TEMPERATURE: Intermediate to cool, with a low of 50°F and never above 80°F

HUMIDITY: High, with good air circulation

MOISTURE: Keep moist all year, ideally with clean rainwater, taking care to avoid extremes of wet and dry.

GROWING MEDIUM: A or C

FERTILIZER: Sparingly, and not at all during periods of stress (such as during warm temperatures)

PLANT SHOWN: Blooming in summer in a 4-inch pot

Masdevallia
Marguerite

MILTASSIA HYBRID

×*MILTASSIA* CHARLES M. FITCH 'AMETHYST'

A man-made genus created by crossing Miltoniopsis *and* Brassia

The 'Amethyst' cultivar of ×*Miltassia* is one of the most impressive achievements in orchid breeding in the latter part of the twentieth century. It is a cross between *Brassia verrucosa* and *Miltoniopsis* (commonly known as *Miltonia spectabilis*). ×*Miltassia* has quickly been recognized as a truly stellar orchid, one that grows vigorously, blooms on and off all year, and is glorious to behold. It is a reliable confidence builder for beginners and the fragrant blooms on long inflorescences can reliably last for weeks.

Charles M. Fitch is one of the best-known plants of ×*Miltassia*. Its all-around superb performance makes it memorable, but its popularity is surely due in part to the fact that it bears the name of one of the orchid world's living heroes. Fitch not only photographs orchids exquisitely (frequently for publications of the American Orchid Society), but he also grows and breeds them with equal success.

These plants do need stronger light than does *Miltoniopsis,* and will prosper in the company of the usual occupants of mostly sunny quarters, such as *Cattleya, Oncidium, Dendrobium,* and *Cymbidium.*

TYPE: Epiphyte

GROWTH HABIT: Sympodial

ORIGINS: Tropical America

BLOOMING SEASON: Fall, or almost any time of year

LIGHT: Medium to high; outdoors, in a little less sun than for *Cattleyas;* indoors in a sunny window, or under multiple fluorescents or high-intensity light

TEMPERATURE: Intermediate, with winter nighttime low of 60°F, maximum highs to 85°F

HUMIDITY: Medium to high, with good air circulation

MOISTURE: Water freely during spring and fall, somewhat less in the coldest, darkest times of year, but never let plant become so dry as to cause pseudobulbs to shrivel

GROWING MEDIUM: A

FERTILIZER: Lightly, frequently, regularly during spring and summer

PLANT SHOWN: Blooming in fall in an 8-inch pot

Miltassia
hybrid

MILTONIDIUM HYBRID

×*MILTONIDIUM* ISSAKU NAGATA 'VOLCANO QUEEN'
(*ONCIDIUM LEUCOCHILUM* × *MILTONIOPSIS WARSCEWICZII*)

A hybrid genus that combines Miltoniopsis *and* Oncidium

A part from its hybrid vigor, this plant resembles both parents, combining the leafiness and showy flowers of the pansy orchid (*Miltoniopsis spectabilis*) with the large, ovoid pseudobulbs and wiry, many-flowered inflorescence of *Oncidium*. Moreover, the long-lasting inflorescence stands tall enough to counterbalance the mass of plant and pot without towering higher than can be seen without a ladder.

The parent *Oncidium leucochilum,* a rare species found in Mexico, Honduras, and Guatemala, was first collected in 1835. It bears flowers with yellow-green petals and speckled brown sepals on an inflorescence, growing up to 10 feet tall, that first appears in winter and can take almost a year to completely flower itself out. The grassy leaves grow to 2 feet.

The other parent, *Miltoniopsis warscewiczii,* originates in Costa Rica. Blooming in winter, its pale pink or white flowers reach almost 3 inches in diameter and grow on an inflorescence about the same length as its pale green leaves, to 10 inches long.

TYPE: Epiphyte

GROWTH HABIT: Sympodial

ORIGINS: Tropical America

BLOOMING SEASON: Winter–spring

LIGHT: Medium to high; outdoors, with enough filtering of direct sun through midday to prevent leaf scorch; indoors in a sunny window, or under multiple fluorescents or high-intensity light

TEMPERATURE: Intermediate, with nighttime minimum of 55°–60°F, year-round maximum of 85°F

HUMIDITY: Medium to high, and always with good air circulation

MOISTURE: Water freely during active growth in spring and summer, somewhat less in fall and winter, but never let plant become so dry as to shrivel the pseudobulbs

GROWING MEDIUM: A

FERTILIZER: Lightly, frequently during spring and summer

PLANT SHOWN: Blooming in spring in a 5-inch pot

Miltonidium
hybrid

MILTONIOPSIS HYBRID

(ALEXANDRE DUMAS × MERRIMAN) ×
(AMBRÉ × HUDSON BAY)
(SOMETIMES CALLED *MILTONIA*)

Genus name means "resembling a Miltonia"

To all eyes save those of the most devoted fancier of the true pansies (which belong to the genus *Viola* and are members of the violet family), miltoniopsis, commonly known as pansy orchids, outshine their namesakes. The arrangement of contrasting colors in true pansy flowers is often referred to as a "face"; in *Miltoniopsis* it is termed a "mask." And while the flowers in both genera are often described as "velvety," those of *Miltoniopsis* last weeks longer, up to a month or more on the plants (but for a disappointingly brief time if cut). With light fragrance and graceful inflorescences of five to seven or more flowers, each carried to stand free of the others, it's easy to see why amateur growers find this orchid irresistible.

When cultivating miltoniopsis, care must be taken to avoid extremes of wet and dry. They will decline slowly if dried out severely, and die quickly from rot if left standing in water or overfertilized. Temperatures ranging between cool and intermediate are preferable, with 45°F being a winter low and 75°F a summer high. A basement fluorescent-light garden in a home with central heating and cooling can provide an ideal place for these small orchid plants.

TYPE: Epiphyte

GROWTH HABIT: Sympodial

ORIGINS: Costa Rica, Panama, Venezuela, Ecuador, Colombia, western Brazil, Peru, Bolivia

BLOOMING SEASON: Spring, or at almost any time of year

LIGHT: Low to medium; outdoors, with shade; indoors in a partly shaded window, or under fluorescents or high-intensity light

TEMPERATURE: Intermediate to cool, with a low range of 45°–60°F, maximum highs to 70°–75°F

HUMIDITY: High, and always with good air circulation

MOISTURE: Keep evenly moist, a bit less so in winter

GROWING MEDIUM: A

FERTILIZER: 20-20-20 at half strength every two weeks during spring and summer, once a month in fall and winter

PLANT SHOWN: Blooming in summer in a 6-inch pot

Miltoniopsis
hybrid

MILTONIOPSIS HYBRID

JEAN SABOURIN VULCAN AM/AOS
(GENUS SOMETIMES CALLED *MILTONIA*)

Genus name means "resembling a Miltonia*"*

The Jean Sabourin hybrids are known and prized for the so-called "waterfall patterns" found in their masks. When Vulcan, the recipient of an Award of Merit from the Royal Horticultural Society, is permitted to multiply, it will form a sizable clump of pseudo-bulbs and can put on one of the most memorable shows imaginable.

These small orchid plants won't tolerate extremes of wet and dry. They will decline slowly if routinely dried out severely, and die quickly from rot if left standing in water or overfertilized. Temperatures ranging between cool and intermediate are preferable, with 45°F being a winter low and 75°F a summer high. A fluorescent-light garden in a home with central heating and cooling can provide an ideal environment.

To all eyes—save those of the most devoted fancier of the true pansies (*Viola* spp.)—miltoniopsis, commonly known as pansy orchids, outshine their namesakes. And while the flowers in both genera are often described as "velvety," those of *Miltoniopsis* last weeks longer, up to a month or more on the plants (but for a disappointingly brief time if cut), and some are delightfully fragrant.

TYPE: Epiphyte

GROWTH HABIT: Sympodial

ORIGINS: Costa Rica, Panama, Venezuela, Ecuador, Colombia; also western Brazil, Peru, Bolivia

BLOOMING SEASON: Spring, or at almost any time of year

LIGHT: Low to medium; outdoors, with shade; indoors in a partly shaded window, or under fluorescents or high-intensity light

TEMPERATURE: Intermediate to cool, with lows of 45–60°F and highs of 70–75°F

HUMIDITY: High, and always with good air circulation

MOISTURE: Always keep evenly moist; water a bit less in winter

GROWING MEDIUM: A

FERTILIZER: 20-20-20 at half-strength every two weeks during spring and summer, once a month in fall and winter

PLANT SHOWN: Blooming in summer in a 6-inch pot

Miltoniopsis
hybrid

MILTONIOPSIS HYBRID

MILTONIOPSIS HUDSON BAY 'ROYALE DREAM' ×
MILTONIOPSIS BUTTERFLY 'YELLOW FLASH'
(GENUS SOMETIMES CALLED *MILTONIA*)

The genus name means "resembling a Miltonia"

This large-flowered seedling has a complex parentage, but the result of crossing cultivars ('Royale Dream' and 'Yellow Flash') is a glorious bloom, 3 to 4 inches in diameter, that combines pale yellow and vivid, velvety dark red. The inflorescence may carry from one to a half dozen or more flowers, often appearing together in a state of perfection for two weeks or more. The plant has ovoid pseudobulbs, 1 to 2 inches tall, topped by long, graceful, folded leaves, which grow up to 12 inches long by 2 inches wide. These can rise up and then droop lightly at the tips.

TYPE: Epiphyte

GROWTH HABIT: Sympodial

ORIGINS: Parts of southern Central America and western South America

BLOOMING SEASON: Spring, or at almost any time of year

LIGHT: Outdoors with shade; indoors in partly shaded window, under fluorescents or high intensity light

TEMPERATURE: Intermediate to cool, with a low range of 45°–60°F, a maximum of 70°–75°F

HUMIDITY: High, always with good air circulation

MOISTURE: Always evenly moist, a bit less so in winter

GROWING MEDIUM: A

FERTILIZER: 20-20-20 at half-strength every two weeks during spring and summer, once a month in fall and winter

PLANT SHOWN: Blooming in spring in a 5-inch pot

Miltoniopsis
hybrid

MILTONIOPSIS HYBRID

MILTONIOPSIS RON HAWLEY ×
EDWIDGE SABOURIN PINK SURPRISE
(SOMETIMES CALLED *MILTONIA*)

Genus name means "resembling a Miltonia"

This seedling has flowers so heavenly that it runs the risk of being mistaken for fakes made fiendishly lifelike by the artful shaping of silk or porcelain. The large flowers will last best on the plants in bright but cool light (avoid direct sun or placement within the obvious glow of heat that comes from an electric light), in a place with moderate temperatures and free of all drafts.

This orchid is very sensitive to drying out—flowers can wither in a matter of hours. Check the plant daily to establish moisture needs. Also avoid haphazard watering, especially when the growing container is placed inside a decorative waterproof one. In this situation, it is preferable to remove the plant in its growing pot to a sink, where it can be drenched and completely drained.

The Ron Hawley side of this orchid is derived from a cross of Limelight × Jules Hye de Crom; Edwidge Sabourin is the result of a cross of Emotion × *Miltoniopsis vexillaria* (pink-blushed and -lined white flowers with a prominent yellow eye); Pink Surprise contributes further, regrouping and concentrating the rose-pink color into a band across the upper part of the flower.

TYPE: Epiphyte

GROWTH HABIT: Sympodial

ORIGINS: Costa Rica, Panama, Venezuela, Ecuador, Colombia, western Brazil, Peru, Bolivia

BLOOMING SEASON: Spring, or at almost any time of year

LIGHT: Low to medium; outdoors, with shade; indoors in a partly shaded window, or under fluorescents or high-intensity light

TEMPERATURE: Intermediate to cool, with a low range of 45°–60°F, maximum highs to 70°–75°F

HUMIDITY: High, and always with good air circulation

MOISTURE: Keep evenly moist, a bit less so in winter

GROWING MEDIUM: A

FERTILIZER: 20-20-20 at half strength every two weeks during spring and summer, once a month in fall and winter

PLANT SHOWN: Blooming in summer in a 3-inch pot

Miltoniopsis
hybrid

MILTONIOPSIS HYBRID

MILTONIOPSIS YOSHIKO TEMPO
(SOMETIMES CALLED *MILTONIA*)

Genus name means "resembling a Miltonia"

When they first open, the flowers of this hybrid from Japan are only about half the size they will become in a few days. The color, as though faded by the increase in size, also pales from a medium rose-lavender to a paler lavender-pink with a vivid dark red mask.

A plant of the dimension shown will typically bloom to this extent when established in a 4-inch plastic pot, which can then be slipped inside a slightly larger decorative container for the duration of the month-long flower show. Plastic pots are recommended for miltoniopsis because they are very sensitive to inconsistent watering or overwatering. They will decline slowly if routinely dried out between waterings, and for this reason many orchidists grow them in plastic pots, which hold moisture better than unglazed clay pots.

Conversely, miltoniopsis die quickly from rot if left standing in water. They are also sensitive to overfertilizing, especially in the fall and winter. Temperatures ranging between cool and intermediate are preferable, with 45°F being a winter low and 75°F a summer high. A basement fluorescent-light garden in a home with central heating and cooling can provide an ideal place for these small orchid plants.

TYPE: Epiphyte

GROWTH HABIT: Sympodial

ORIGINS: Costa Rica, Panama, Venezuela, Ecuador, Colombia, western Brazil, Peru, Bolivia

BLOOMING SEASON: Spring, or at almost any time of year

LIGHT: Low to medium; outdoors, with shade; indoors in a partly shaded window, or under fluorescents or high-intensity light

TEMPERATURE: Intermediate to cool, with a low range of 45°–60°F, maximum highs to 70°–75°F

HUMIDITY: High, and always with good air circulation

MOISTURE: Keep evenly moist, a bit less so in winter

GROWING MEDIUM: A

FERTILIZER: 20-20-20 at half strength every two weeks during spring and summer, once a month in fall and winter

PLANT SHOWN: Blooming in spring in a 4-inch pot

Miltoniopsis
hybrid

NEOFINETIA FALCATA

NEOFINETIA FALCATA 'BLANCO'

Genus named for Achille Finet (1862–1913), a French botanist
who specialized in the orchids of China and Japan

T he only species in the genus *Nicofinetia, N. falcata* is named for the falcate habit of the leaves, which strongly curve sideways like a sickle.

The powerfully sweet-scented flowers have unusually long pedicels and ovaries. In cultivation, many clones have been selected based on variations in leaf shape, spur length, and variegation. A pink-flowered clone, however, is rarely seen outside Japan. The cultivar 'Blanco' is pristinely white and slightly larger in all aspects than the species.

N. falcata grows 3 to 6 inches tall. The fragrant, long-lasting flowers are pure white, often turning golden in their last days; these have slender, 2-inch-long spurs, giving the spikes an airy, spidery effect. When hybridized with species of *Ascocentrum*, ×*Ascofinetia* is the result, a man-made genus esteemed for its performance as a potted plant.

TYPE: Epiphyte

GROWTH HABIT: Monopodial

ORIGINS: Japan, Korea, and the Ryukyu Islands

BLOOMING SEASON: Spring–summer

LIGHT: Medium; outdoors, with some shade; indoors in a partly sunny window, or under multiple fluorescents or high-intensity light

TEMPERATURE: Intermediate to warm, with winter lows of 58°–62°F

HUMIDITY: Medium to high, with good air circulation

MOISTURE: Keep moist during spring and summer, less so as growth subsides, but never allow to become so dry as to shrivel the leaves or pseudobulbs.

GROWING MEDIUM: A

FERTILIZER: Lightly, frequently, regularly in spring and summer

PLANT SHOWN: Blooming in summer in a 6-inch pot

Neofinetia
falcata

NEOSTYLIS HYBRID

×*NEOSTYLIS*
(*NEOFINETIA FALCATA* × *RHYNCOSTYLIS COELESTIS*)

A man-made genus, created by crossing Neofinetia *and* Rhyncostylis, *and first reported 1965*

Beautiful form makes this orchid perfect for any collection of small plants. Like most diminutive orchids, its appeal stems from the size and habit, which allows for easy maintenance through cold weather under multiple fluorescents or high-intensity light.

The flowers of the plant shown have white petals and sepals; the lip is blushed pink-lavender-blue. The inflorescence rises from the base of a mature leaf and stands 3 to 4 inches high, with nine flowers facing in all directions. They are long-lasting, up to a month or more, and emit a definite fragrance, almost petrochemical at first, but giving way to a certain sweetness. This particular plant is also prized for its ability to bloom twice yearly.

TYPE: Epiphyte

GROWTH HABIT: Monopodial

ORIGINS: *Neofinetia* from Japan, Korea, the Ryukyu Islands; *Rhyncostylis* from Thailand

BLOOMING SEASON: Summer–fall

LIGHT: Medium; outdoors, with some shade; indoors in a partly sunny window, or under multiple fluorescents or high-intensity light

TEMPERATURE: Intermediate to warm, with winter lows of 58°–62°F

HUMIDITY: Medium to high, with good air circulation

MOISTURE: Keep moist during spring and summer, less so as growth subsides, but never allow to become so dry as to shrivel the leaves or pseudobulbs

GROWING MEDIUM: A

FERTILIZER: Lightly, frequently, regularly in spring and summer

PLANT SHOWN: Blooming in fall in a 4-inch pot

Neostylis
hybrid

ODONTIODA HYBRID

×*ODONTIODA* SUSI 'SCARLET PASSION' AM/AOS
(*ODONTOGLOSSUM BICTONIENSE* × ×*ODONTIODA*
[*COCHLIODA* × *ODONTOGLOSSUM*] FEUERBALL)

A hybrid genus combining Cochlioda *and* Odontoglossum

In 1906 the red of the *Cochlioda* orchid was combined with the gorgeous sprays of the *Odontoglossum* to produce this popular hybrid genus. Although some of the *Cochlioda* progenitors are now listed under *Symphyglossum,* crosses with *Odontoglossum* remain classified as ×*Odontioda* to avoid further chaos from jumbled nomenclature. The *Odontoglossum* parent of the plant shown has also been reclassified as *Lemboglossum bictoniense.*

The award-winning Susi 'Scarlet Passion' is marvelously fragrant, a trait probably inherited from its *Odontoglossum* parent. Its flowers are pale green or yellow-green, banded or spotted red-brown.

×*Odontioda* enjoys cool to intermediate temperatures. This orchid won't mind a winter drop to 45° from 55°F, but don't push the summer limit much above 75°F. Eastern or southern exposure is best for the medium light it prefers. The high humidity of a greenhouse is a perfect atmosphere for ×*Odontioda* and will encourage many blooms, but even pebble humidity trays under their pots around the house will be much appreciated. Water and fertilize generously all year, and don't let the plants dry too much between waterings.

TYPE: Epiphyte

GROWTH HABIT: Sympodial

ORIGINS: Tropical America

BLOOMING SEASON: Spring–summer

LIGHT: Medium; outdoors, with ample filtering of sun's direct rays through midday to prevent leaf scorch; indoors in or near a sunny window, or under multiple fluorescents or high-intensity light

TEMPERATURE: Cool to intermediate, with winter nighttime lows of 45°–55°F, summer days ideally not higher than 75°–80°F

HUMIDITY: High, with good air circulation; in the house, use a humidifier as well as pebble humidity trays

MOISTURE: Water freely in all seasons, permitting plants to dry only slightly between waterings

GROWING MEDIUM: A

FERTILIZER: Lightly, frequently, regularly, except in fall and early winter

PLANT SHOWN: Blooming in spring in a 6-inch pot

Odontioda
hybrid

ODONTOCIDIUM HYBRID

×*ODONTOCIDIUM* HANS NEUENHAUS 'GRANDE'
(*ONCIDIUM TIGRINUM* 'GRANDIFLORUM' ×
ODONTOGLOSSUM MOSELLE)

A hybrid genus combining Odontoglossum *and* Oncidium

The hearty orchid ×*Odontocidium* Hans Neuenhaus 'Grande' is a highly evolved, exceptionally outstanding performer. The vigor of the 'Grande' plant and the showiness of its long-lasting bloom period make this one of the most worthy orchids to be meristemmed and mass-marketed. In numerous ways, it's more suited to this treatment than many species orchids (some of which are endangered) that have been recommended to the amateur.

The vigorous pseudobulbs, 2 to 3 inches tall, are decidedly sculptural. The bold leaves, 12 inches tall by 4 inches wide, seem to foretell the long inflorescences, which grow to 2 feet tall. The 5- to 6-inch brown-tigered flowers open one after the other to the very tip, thus affording an extended show of up to two months or more.

A closely allied man-made genus, ×*Wilsonara,* represents the crossing of *Cochlioda* × *Odontoglossum* × *Oncidium.* The flowers of some of these resemble those of the ×*Odontocidium* shown here, except that they may be twice this size in relation to the foliage. Also allied is the man-made genus ×*Vuylstekeara.*

TYPE: Epiphyte

GROWTH HABIT: Sympodial

ORIGINS: Tropical America

BLOOMING SEASON: Winter–spring

LIGHT: Medium; outdoors, with sufficient filtering of sun's direct rays through midday to prevent leaf scorch; indoors in or near a sunny window, or under multiple fluorescents or high-intensity light

TEMPERATURE: Intermediate to cool, with winter nighttime lows of 53°–60°F, summer highs not exceeding 75°–80°F

HUMIDITY: High, and always with free air movement

MOISTURE: Water well, then not again until there has been a slight drying; when the main growth period is over, maintain on the dry side

GROWING MEDIUM: A, with perfect drainage

FERTILIZER: Lightly, frequently in spring and summer

PLANT SHOWN: Blooming in spring in a 6-inch pot

Odontocidium
hybrid

ONCIDIUM HYBRID

ONCIDIUM MAGIC 'HILDES'
(RAINBOW × GOLDEN SUNSET)

Genus name comes from the diminutive form of the Greek word onkos *(swelling),
referring to the fleshy pad on the lip of many species*

This hybrid is called an "equitant" *Oncidium,* from its habit of putting forth symmetrical fans of narrow, deeply grooved leaves in one plane to either side of the rhizome. The leaves are only 2 to 4 inches tall and multiply quickly. The erect inflorescence grows from between the two sets of stacked leaves and may rise 18 inches high or more, and branch out. Flower blossoms cluster at the end of the stalk.

Equitant oncidiums can survive temperatures up to 100°F if air circulation is good. They particularly appreciate a warm, humid daytime environment and daily watering and misting, and should not be exposed to temperatures lower than 64°F at night. They need constant air movement (fans are a good idea) and very good drainage. Give them clay pots with an open mix of medium bark and charcoal, and keep them fertilized with a high-nitrogen formula—but only when they're actively growing.

It is widely believed that the equitant species, about 22 in all, belong in a separate genus called *Tolumnia.* If this reassignment occurs, however, those species will still be commonly listed as *Oncidium.*

TYPE: Epiphyte

GROWTH HABIT: Sympodial

ORIGINS: Caribbean region

BLOOMING SEASON: Fall–winter, or at almost any time of year

LIGHT: Medium; outdoors, with sufficient filtering of direct sunlight through midday to prevent leaf scorch; indoors in or near a sunny window, or under multiple fluorescents or high-intensity light

TEMPERATURE: Intermediate to warm, preferably not colder than 60°F in any season

HUMIDITY: Medium to high, with free air movement

MOISTURE: Water well in all seasons, but allow to dry slightly between waterings; avoid extremes of wet and dry; indoors, mist on days when watering is not required

GROWING MEDIUM: A, or mounted on cork or tree-fern

FERTILIZER: Lightly, frequently, regularly with 30-10-10 in spring and summer or during active growth

PLANT SHOWN: Blooming in fall in a 2½-inch pot

Oncidium hybrid

ONCIDIUM HYBRID

ONCIDIUM ORNITHORHYNCHUM 'PODD' × 'GORGEOUS'

Genus name comes from the diminutive form of the Greek word onkos (swelling),
referring to the fleshy pad on the lip of many species

This hybrid—like the species from which it comes—forms clusters if not miniature clouds of small purple, pink, or white blossoms with golden-yellow calluses on inflorescences that may extend to 2 feet long. The blossoms are a little smaller than an inch in diameter and give off a generosity of perfume that can fill a sizable room during the warm part of the day.

The leaves arch and grow to about 9 to 15 inches long by 1½ inches wide. The species is closely related to *Oncidium cheirophorum,* though the two are easily differentiated when the latter's yellow flowers are in bloom.

O. ornithorhynchum was first described by F.H.A. von Humboldt, A. Bonpland, and C. S. Knuth in 1815. Humboldt had discovered the plant in Michoacan State, Mexico, during his travels in the mountains near Valladolid. The species was first cultivated contemporaneously by James Bateman, using Guatemalan specimens collected by George Ure Skinner, and by Messrs. Loddiges, using Mexican specimens collected by Count Karwinsky.

TYPE: Epiphyte

GROWTH HABIT: Sympodial

ORIGINS: Mexico, Guatemala, El Salvador, Costa Rica

BLOOMING SEASON: Summer–fall

LIGHT: Part sun to part shade; outdoors, with enough filtering of sunlight through midday to prevent leaf scorch; indoors in or near a sunny window, or under multiple fluorescents or high-intensity light; avoid northern exposure except while plant is actually in bloom

TEMPERATURE: Intermediate, with winter nights no lower than 55°–60°F

HUMIDITY: Moderate, with good air movement

MOISTURE: Water well in all seasons, but allow to dry between waterings; after newest growths are mature, maintain quite dry and somewhat cooler for 8 to 12 weeks

GROWING MEDIUM: A

FERTILIZER: Lightly, frequently, consistently during active growth

PLANT SHOWN: Blooming in fall in a 5-inch pot

Oncidium
hybrid

ONCIDIUM HYBRID

ONCIDIUM SHARRY BABY 'SWEET FRAGRANCE' (JAMIE SUTTON × HONOLULU)

Genus name comes from the diminutive form of the Greek word onkos *(swelling), referring to the fleshy pad on the lip of many species*

This primarily summer- or fall-blooming hybrid is quite simply a fantastic orchid, worthy of cherishing. It's easy to grow, easy to bloom, and wonderfully fragrant. A single plant will perfume an entire room with countless flowers over a period of up to three months, on one to several inflorescences growing to 3 to 4 feet high. Through meri-cloning, this has rapidly become one of the most popular orchids available.

Sharry Baby's pseudobulbs are big—to 3 inches tall—and topped by handsome, thick, medium dark green leaves more than an inch wide and up to a foot long. Individual flowers, about 1 inch wide by 1½ inches tall, have maroon petals and sepals that show off a ruffly pale pink-white lip (it's easy to imagine a human figure in these charming blossoms).

Like Gowers Ramsey (see page 146), another widely admired oncidium, Sharry Baby has the generous habit of appearing to be in bloom all the time. In fact, if several plants are in a collection and all grow reasonably well, one or more may be in bloom literally year-round.

TYPE: Epiphyte

GROWTH HABIT: Sympodial

ORIGINS: Central America

BLOOMING SEASON: Summer–fall

LIGHT: Part sun to part shade; outdoors, with enough filtering of sunlight through midday to prevent leaf scorch; indoors in or near a sunny window, or under multiple fluorescents or high-intensity light; avoid northern exposure except while plant is actually in bloom

TEMPERATURE: Intermediate, with winter nights no lower than 55°–60°F

HUMIDITY: Moderate, with good air movement

MOISTURE: Water well in all seasons, but allow to dry between waterings; after newest growths are mature, maintain quite dry and somewhat cooler for 8 to 12 weeks

GROWING MEDIUM: A

FERTILIZER: Lightly, frequently, consistently during active growth

PLANT SHOWN: Blooming in fall in a 5-inch pot

Oncidium
hybrid

ONCIDIUM HYBRID

ONCIDIUM SWEET SUGAR 'EMPEROR'

Genus name comes from the diminutive form of the Greek word onkos *(swelling),
referring to the fleshy pad on the lip of many species*

Sweet Sugar 'Emperor' and the similar 'Angel' cultivar can put on a
blooming exhibition that lasts and lasts. They can be purchased in
full bud, at the moment the first flowers are beginning to open,
then brought home and watched with great pleasure as they gradually
open more and more until finally, after a month or two, the show is at
full tilt. Then as the oldest begin to wither, the youngest carry on for
another couple of months.

Both 'Emperor' and 'Angel' (recipient of an SM from the Japanese
Orchid Growers Association) are notably compact in habit, which makes
them highly suitable for many amateur growers and relatively easy to
manage through distribution and shipment over long distances.

Oncidium Sweet Sugar is from a cross of Aloha × *O. varicosum* that
was registered in 1990. The much-awarded *O. varicosum* parent bears
copious, rich yellow blossoms in branching sprays. Hailing from Bolivia,
Brazil, and Paraguay, *O. varicosum* puts out inflorescences 3 to 5 feet
long with flowers that last at least six to eight weeks. Although too tall
in bloom to manage in the usual fluorescent-light garden, the plants
actually do well in a setup with four 40-watt tubes.

TYPE: Epiphyte

GROWTH HABIT: Sympodial

ORIGINS: Species originally from South America

BLOOMING SEASON: Spring–fall, or at almost any time of year

LIGHT: Part sun to part shade; outdoors, with enough filtering of sunlight through midday to prevent leaf scorch; indoors in or near a sunny window, or under multiple fluorescents or high-intensity light; avoid northern exposure except while plant is in bloom

TEMPERATURE: Intermediate, with winter nights no lower than 55°–60°F

HUMIDITY: Moderate, with good air movement

MOISTURE: Water well in all seasons, but allow to dry between waterings; after newest growths are mature, maintain quite dry and somewhat cooler for 8 to 12 weeks

GROWING MEDIUM: A

FERTILIZER: Lightly, frequently, consistently during active growth

PLANT SHOWN: Blooming in spring in a 4-inch pot

Oncidium
hybrid

ONCIDIUM ONUSTUM

Genus name is from the Greek onkos *(swelling) in the diminutive form,*
referring to the fleshy pad on the lip of many species

What this orchid may lack in flash, it more than makes up for in purity of form and color. And since the plant does well left alone to form a cluster of pseudobulbs, it's relatively low maintenance.

A fall-blooming species, *Oncidium onustum* has 1-inch pseudobulbs that cluster to fill a 4-inch pot. This habit results in the production of numerous inflorescences up to 15 to 18 inches high, each with up to 21 diminutive flowers in one relatively small pot. They last a month or more and are essentially medium yellow, without any other discernible colors or noticeable markings.

A popular offspring of this species is Honey Bee, which represents a cross of Memoria Harold Starkey × *O. onustum. O. sphacelatum* × *O. onustum* has produced another outstanding performer, Butterball.

TYPE: Epiphyte

GROWTH HABIT: Sympodial

ORIGINS: Dry regions of Ecuador and Peru

BLOOMING SEASON: Fall

LIGHT: Part sun to part shade; outdoors, with enough filtering of sun's hot rays through midday to prevent leaf scorch; indoors in or near a sunny window, or under multiple fluorescents or high-intensity light; avoid northern exposure except while actually in bloom

TEMPERATURE: Intermediate, with a winter nighttime minimum of 55°–60°F

HUMIDITY: Moderate, with good air movement

MOISTURE: Water well in all seasons but allow to dry between waterings; after newest growths are mature, maintain dry and somewhat cooler for 8 to 12 weeks

GROWING MEDIUM: A

FERTILIZER: Lightly, frequently during active growth

PLANT SHOWN: Blooming in fall in a 4-inch pot

*Oncidium
onustum*

OTAARA HYBRID

×OTAARA KRULL SMITH 'RIVERBEND' AM/AOS

A quadrigeneric man-made hybrid

(Brassavola × Broughtonia × Cattleya × Laelia) *created by Krull Smith in 1985*

This gorgeous orchid is well known as Krull Smith 'Riverbend.' Most admirers don't realize the complexity of its lineage and often mistake it for a "big cattleya." It is, in fact, a cross of ×*Brassolaeliocattleya* Oconee × ×*Cattleytonia* Keith Roth.

Any collector who loves cattleya orchids will have great appreciation of ×*Otaara* and will not consider a collection complete without at least one specimen. The plants themselves get on well under conditions where cattleyas thrive.

'Riverbend' is among the world's most beautiful orchids. Individual flowers can measure up to 6 inches across, and the large, ruffled, velvety-textured lip is possessed of strong vigor. The plant grows to 12 inches tall, and has relatively slender pseudobulbs and leaves.

TYPE: Epiphyte, lithophyte

GROWTH HABIT: Sympodial

ORIGINS: Hybrid

BLOOMING SEASON: Spring–summer

LIGHT: Medium to high; outdoors, with sufficient filtering of direct rays to avoid sunburn; indoors in a sunny window, or under multiple fluorescents or high-intensity light

TEMPERATURE: Intermediate, with a minimum temperature of 55°–60°F in winter

HUMIDITY: Medium to high, with good air circulation

MOISTURE: Water generously during spring and summer, but let dry a bit between waterings; water less in fall and winter, but never allow to become so dry as to shrivel the pseudobulbs

GROWING MEDIUM: A

FERTILIZER: Lightly, frequently, consistently in spring and summer, less in fall and winter

PLANT SHOWN: Blooming in spring in a 7-inch pot

Otaara hybrid

PAPHIOPEDILUM BELLATULUM 'LOTSA DOTS'

(SYN. *CYPRIPEDIUM BELLATULUM*)

Popularly called lady's-slipper or Venus's-slipper orchid,
for the shape of the lip; the genus name is from the Greek Paphos
(a city on Cyprus where a temple dedicated to Venus stands) and pedilon *(slipper)*

When indoor gardeners began to grow plants under banks of fluorescent lights after World War II, *Paphiopedilum bellatulum* was one of the first orchids to gain popularity. It's a showy and exceptionally exotic orchid that sends up flowers only an inch or so above the low-growing leaves. The conformation is ideal for the fluorescent-light garden.

The large, rounded lady's-slipper flowers appear singly, each about 3 inches wide, and white with liberally scattered purple spots. 'Lotsa Dots' was chosen from a large number of plants propagated from collected specimens for the exceptional intensity, large number, and overall visual impact of its dots. The elliptic-shaped leaves are speckled green-gray; the plant grows to about 6 inches across.

Paphiopedilum is closely related to *Cypripedium,* as are *Selenipedium* and *Phragmipedium,* the other genera of slipper orchids. In the past, all four of these genera have been lumped together as *Cypripedium.*

TYPE: Terrestrial; occasionally epiphytic

GROWTH HABIT: Sympodial

ORIGINS: Burma, Thailand

BLOOMING SEASON: Late spring to early summer, or at almost any time of year if grown under lights

LIGHT: Low; outdoors, in mostly shade; indoors near almost any bright window, or under fluorescent or high-intensity light

TEMPERATURE: Intermediate, with winter nights no cooler than 55°–60°F

HUMIDITY: High, constant; a humidity tray will augment supply

MOISTURE: Keep moist at all times; these orchids have no means of storing water

GROWING MEDIUM: A or B; in small, deep pots with room for the extensive root system; these plants appreciate frequent repotting

FERTILIZER: Lightly, frequently, consistently during growth season

PLANT SHOWN: Blooming in spring in a 4-inch pot

Paphiopedilum
bellatulum 'lotsa dots'

PAPHIOPEDILUM CHAMBERLAINIANUM

(SYN. *PAPHIOPEDILUM VICTORIAREGINA;* SOMETIMES PLACED
IN THE SUBGENUS *COCHLOPETALUM*)

*Genus is named after Paphos (a city on Cyprus where a temple dedicated to Venus stands)
and* pedilon *(slipper); popularly called lady's-slipper or Venus's-slipper orchids,
for the shape of the lip*

Unlike the more commonly grown lady's-slipper orchids that send up one flower at a time, this plant produces up to 30, one by one in zigzag sequence along the inflorescence. This habit makes *Paphiopedilum chamberlainianum* a thrifty specimen that is always in bloom. It's a beautiful orchid to display in any flattering, soft light and can look particularly attractive on a library table with shelves of books as a background.

The flowers, up to 3 inches across, are showy with a greenish to white dorsal sepal striped lengthwise in dark brown and spotted purple at the base. The wide-mouthed "slipper" of the flower is pink, generously spotted with purple. The oval leaves are dark green, to 8 inches long by a third as much wide, and are often mottled in a lighter green.

F. Sander was the first to cultivate this orchid and to describe it in 1892. He designated it *Cypripedium victoria-regina* to honor Queen Victoria.

TYPE: Terrestrial

GROWTH HABIT: Sympodial

ORIGINS: Sumatra

BLOOMING SEASON: Spring–summer, or at any time of year, especially in a fluorescent-light garden

LIGHT: Bright diffuse, with consistent shading from direct sunlight; excellent under fluorescents or high-intensity light

TEMPERATURE: Intermediate, with a winter nighttime minimum of 55°–60°F

HUMIDITY: High, constant; a humidity tray helps

MOISTURE: Keep moist at all times; these orchids have no means of storing water and should not become dry

GROWING MEDIUM: A or B; in small, deep pots with room for the extensive root system

FERTILIZER: Lightly, frequently during active growth

PLANT SHOWN: Blooming in spring in a 6-inch pot

*Paphiopedilum
chamberlainianum*

PAPHIOPEDILUM HIRSUTISSIMUM 'PETER'

(SYN. *CYPRIPEDIUM HIRSUTISSIMUM*)

Genus is named after Paphos (a city on Cyprus where a temple dedicated to Venus stands) and pedilon *(slipper); popularly called lady's-slipper or Venus's-slipper orchids, for the shape of the lip*

Named for a nephew in the Hausermann family of orchid growers, 'Peter' offers an elegant green flower with a purple dorsal sepal and horizontally spreading, slightly twisted pink petals, 6 to 7 inches across. This bloom stands 6 to 12 inches tall, or slightly above the leaves, and will last two to six weeks. The vigorous plant produces a plentiful supply of evergreen leaves, each 8 to 12 inches long by 2 inches wide, which make a handsome mass of foliage even when there are no flowers to admire.

A lady's-slipper orchid such as 'Peter' has wonderful presence when it's elevated to eye level. In bloom, the plants are often the ideal size for placing on a desk or worktable, or by the bedside.

TYPE: Terrestrial

GROWTH HABIT: Sympodial

ORIGINS: India

BLOOMING SEASON: Spring–summer, or at any time of year, especially in a fluorescent-light garden

LIGHT: Bright diffuse, with consistent shading from direct sunlight; excellent under fluorescents or high-intensity light

TEMPERATURE: Intermediate, with a winter nighttime minimum of 55°–60°F

HUMIDITY: High, constant; use a humidity tray

MOISTURE: Keep moist at all times; these orchids have no means of storing water and should not become dry

GROWING MEDIUM: A or B, in small, deep pots with room for the extensive root system

FERTILIZER: Lightly, frequently during growth season

PLANT SHOWN: Blooming in spring in a 7-inch pot

*Paphiopedilum
hirsutissimum* 'Peter'

PAPHIOPEDILUM HYBRID

PAPHIOPEDILUM COOS 'JUNE BLOOM'
(P. PRAESTANS × P. CHAMBERLAINIANUM)

Genus is named after Paphos (a city on Cyprus where a temple dedicated to Venus stands)
and pedilon *(slipper); popularly called lady's-slipper or Venus's-slipper orchids,*
for the shape of the lip

This superb hybrid multibloomer carries up to 30 flowers that open sequentially along the inflorescence. The foliage is outstanding, a perfect foil for the intricately lined, dotted, and furled flower parts. Leaves are dark green, large, long (up to 12 inches long by 2 inches wide), and plentiful, which tends to yield a strong plant capable of producing many blooms over a protracted season.

The individual flowers of 'June Bloom' can measure up to 6 inches across on an inflorescence that may eventually reach to 24 inches long. This orchid greatly benefits from some kind of support. A slender cane inserted into the growing medium, and one or two ties made with raffia, will keep the flowers nicely displayed.

While unsuited to the rank amateur, this orchid is perfect for the serious beginner or even the advanced grower who may have become a bit jaded about more common varieties. It needs constant high humidity and moisture in the growing medium at all times.

TYPE: Terrestrial

GROWTH HABIT: Sympodial

ORIGINS: Java, New Guinea, southeastern Asia

BLOOMING SEASON: Spring–summer, or at any time of year, especially in a fluorescent-light garden

LIGHT: Bright diffuse, with consistent shading from direct sunlight; excellent under fluorescents or high-intensity light

TEMPERATURE: Intermediate, with a winter nighttime minimum of 55°–60°F

HUMIDITY: High, constant; use a humidity tray

MOISTURE: Keep moist at all times; these orchids have no means of storing water and should not become dry

GROWING MEDIUM: A or B, in small, deep pots with room for the extensive root system

FERTILIZER: Lightly, frequently during growth season

PLANT SHOWN: Blooming in spring in a 7-inch pot

Paphiopedilum
hybrid

PAPHIOPEDILUM HYBRID

PAPHIOPEDILUM LYNNLEIGH KOOPOWITZ
(*P. DELENATII* × *P. MALIPOENSE*)

Popularly called lady's-slipper or Venus's-slipper orchid,
for the shape of the lip; the genus name is from the Greek Paphos
(a city on Cyprus where a temple dedicated to Venus stands) and pedilon *(slipper)*

L ynnleigh Koopowitz is a must-have for every serious collector of paphiopedilums, especially those with an affinity for white or pale pink flowers. Less than ten years old, this orchid is already very popular. It was created in 1991 from a cross of two Asian species, and the offspring possesses the most desirable traits of its parents.

The parent *Paphiopedilum delenatii* is originally from North Vietnam and is now possibly eradicated in its wild form. It bears delicate white and pink flowers in early spring, with blooms measuring almost 3 inches across. The leaves are narrow and deeply mottled, about 5 inches long and 2 inches across. The plant enjoys constant high humidity and shade in cool temperatures with plenty of water.

The other parent, *P. malipoense,* from southwestern China, possesses an unusual green flower speckled and veined with purple. The leaves are deeply mottled in green and purple and measure 4 to 10 inches long. Each stem bears a single flower that smells strongly of raspberry.

TYPE: Terrestrial

GROWTH HABIT: Sympodial

ORIGINS: Species parents from North Vietnam and southwestern China

BLOOMING SEASON: Spring–summer, or at any time of year, especially in a fluorescent-light garden

LIGHT: Bright diffuse, with consistent shading from direct sunlight; excellent under fluorescent or high-intensity light

TEMPERATURE: Intermediate, with winter nights no cooler than 55°–60°F

HUMIDITY: High, constant; a humidity tray will augment supply

MOISTURE: Keep moist at all times; these orchids have no means of storing water

GROWING MEDIUM: A or B; in small, deep pots with room for the extensive root system; these plants appreciate frequent repotting

FERTILIZER: Lightly, frequently, consistently during growth season

PLANT SHOWN: Blooming in spring in a 4-inch pot

Paphiopedilum
hybrid

PAPHIOPEDILUM HYBRID

PAPHIOPEDILUM MAUDIAE 'MAGNIFICUM'

Popularly called lady's-slipper or Venus's-slipper orchid,
for the shape of the lip; the genus name is from the Greek Paphos
(a city on Cyprus where a temple dedicated to Venus stands) and pedilon *(slipper)*

The Maudiae paphs are often listed among the best beginner orchids. They are fairly easy to accommodate along with almost any healthy, thriving houseplants. And their habit of blooming twice yearly makes them extremely appealing when compared to orchids that get their act together only once every twelve months.

Paphiopedilum Maudiae 'Magnificum' is one of the best known lady's-slipper orchids. Another popular cultivar is 'The Queen,' which is always reliable and puts on a great show.

×Maudiac is a nineteenth-century hybrid species created by crossing *P. callosum* × *P. lawrenceanum.* It was originally bred using the parents' *alba* types, resulting in a fresh-looking flower with a praying-mantis-green "slipper" and white dorsal sepal, striped green lengthwise. When this orchid was bred using colored specimens of the same parent species, a flower with a purple pouch and a purple striped dorsal sepal was the result.

TYPE: Terrestrial

GROWTH HABIT: Sympodial

ORIGINS: Thailand, Cambodia, Laos, northern Malaya, Borneo

BLOOMING SEASON: Spring–summer, or at any time of year, especially in a fluorescent-light garden

LIGHT: Bright diffuse, with consistent shading from direct sunlight; excellent under fluorescent or high-intensity light

TEMPERATURE: Intermediate, with winter nights no cooler than 55°–60°F

HUMIDITY: High, constant; a humidity tray will augment supply

MOISTURE: Keep moist at all times; these orchids have no means of storing water

GROWING MEDIUM: A or B; in small, deep pots with room for the extensive root system; these plants appreciate frequent repotting

FERTILIZER: Lightly, frequently, consistently during growth season

PLANT SHOWN: Blooming in spring in a 5-inch pot

Paphiopedilum
hybrid

PAPHIOPEDILUM NIVEUM VAR. ANG-THONG 'FANCIFUL'

(SYN. *CYPRIPEDIUM NIVEUM*)

Popularly called lady's-slipper or Venus's-slipper orchid,
for the shape of the lip; the genus name is from the Greek Paphos
(a city on Cyprus where a temple dedicated to Venus stands) and pedilon *(slipper)*

'Fanciful' is one of the finest possible miniature lady's-slipper orchids for the amateur collector and lover of these plants. Perfect for intermediate to warm fluorescent-light gardens, it may well yield two flowerings a year.

The rounded white flowers of *Paphiopedilum niveum* appear one to a stem, usually in late spring and summer. They commonly have a fine mist dotting of purple on the petals, although pure white forms are not unusual. The leaves are narrow, elliptic, and dark green with gray mottling on the surface, purple-blushed on the underside. Paphiopedilums with gray to silver markings on the otherwise green foliage tend to make better houseplants than other varieties.

TYPE: Terrestrial

GROWTH HABIT: Sympodial

ORIGINS: Species parent *P. niveum* from southern Thailand and northern Malaya

BLOOMING SEASON: Spring–summer, or at any time of year, especially in a fluorescent-light garden

LIGHT: Bright diffuse, with consistent shading from direct sunlight; excellent under fluorescent or high-intensity light

TEMPERATURE: Intermediate, with winter nights no cooler than 55°–60°F

HUMIDITY: High, constant; a humidity tray will augment supply

MOISTURE: Keep moist at all times; these orchids have no means of storing water

GROWING MEDIUM: A or B; in small, deep pots with room for the extensive root system; these plants appreciate frequent repotting

FERTILIZER: Lightly, frequently, consistently during growth season

PLANT SHOWN: Blooming in spring in a 3-inch pot

Paphiopedilum niveum
var. ang-thong 'fanciful'

PAPHIOPEDILUM HYBRID

PHAPHIOPEDILUM SUKHAKULII 'BIG BUBBA' × (*P.* SPRING TREE × *P.* VIA JARDIN LUSTROSO)

Popularly called lady's-slipper or Venus's-slipper orchid,
for the shape of the lip; the genus name is from the Greek Paphos
(a city on Cyprus where a temple dedicated to Venus stands) and pedilon *(slipper)*

The extraordinary flowers of this lady's-slipper orchid appear singly atop a short, sturdy stem only 5 to 7 inches above the center of the mature new growth from which it arises. The drooping, narrowly elliptic, mottled green leaves measure to 2 inches across and 5 inches long. The blossom appears in shades of pale green, yellow, or white, with purple-spotted petals, and has a distinct spreading, broad presence.

Paphiopedilum sukhakulii, like the long-popular *P. callosum,* is of fairly easy culture, a trait it has passed along to its progeny. The plant pictured represents a cross of *P. sukhakulii* 'Big Bubba' × [Spring Tree × Via Jardin Lustroso]; both of which are complex hybrids.

The species was discovered by accident in 1964 when it was found as a stowaway in a shipment of *P. callosum* imported from Thailand. It was subsequently described as *P. sukhakulii* in 1965. The species is certainly related to the Burmese *P. wardii,* and it's possible that *P. sukhakulii* may eventually be classified as a subspecies of that.

TYPE: Terrestrial

GROWTH HABIT: Sympodial

ORIGINS: Northeastern Thailand

BLOOMING SEASON: Spring–summer, or at any time of year, especially in a fluorescent-light garden

LIGHT: Bright diffuse, with consistent shading from direct sunlight; excellent under fluorescent or high-intensity light

TEMPERATURE: Intermediate, with winter nights no cooler than 55°–60°F

HUMIDITY: High, constant; a humidity tray will augment supply

MOISTURE: Keep moist at all times; these orchids have no means of storing water

GROWING MEDIUM: B, in small, deep pots with room for the extensive root system; these plants appreciate frequent repotting; oak leaf mold and sandy loam are excellent

FERTILIZER: Lightly, frequently, consistently during growth season

PLANT SHOWN: Blooming in summer in a 4-inch pot

Paphiopedilum
hybrid

PAPHIOPEDILUM HYBRID

PAPHIOPEDILUM VANDA M. PEARMAN 'SOFT SPOTS'

Popularly called lady's-slipper or Venus's-slipper orchid,
for the shape of the lip; the genus name is from the Greek Paphos
(a city on Cyprus where a temple dedicated to Venus stands) and pedilon *(slipper)*

The mottling of the leaf surfaces of this orchid indicate that it will make an excellent houseplant, not requiring the cooler night temperatures sometimes required by paphs with plain dark green leaves.

Both parents, *Paphiopedilum bellatulum* and *P. delenatii,* are extremely popular and widely cultivated, so it's not surprising that Vanda M. Pearman and cultivars such as 'Soft Spots' find a ready supply of admirers and growers ready to give them space and tender loving care.

The beautifully rounded white flowers are softly dotted with pale to light rose-pink. The leaves are short to medium, rounded, and a delight to manage in a window garden or under a fluorescent-light setup for orchids.

A thrifty division should bloom by its second or third season, ideal for a 3- or 4-inch pot, and within a year or two it can fill out a size larger and have enough growths to produce several flowers.

TYPE: Terrestrial

GROWTH HABIT: Sympodial

ORIGINS: *P. bellatulum* from Burma, Thailand; *P. delenatii* from North Vietnam

BLOOMING SEASON: Spring–summer, or at any time of year, especially in a fluorescent-light garden

LIGHT: Bright diffuse, with consistent shading from direct sunlight; excellent under fluorescent or high-intensity light

TEMPERATURE: Intermediate, with winter nights no cooler than 55°–60°F

HUMIDITY: High, constant; a humidity tray will augment supply

MOISTURE: Keep moist at all times; these orchids have no means of storing water

GROWING MEDIUM: A or B; in small, deep pots with room for the extensive root system; these plants appreciate frequent repotting

FERTILIZER: Lightly, frequently, consistently during growth season

PLANT SHOWN: Blooming in spring in a 6-inch pot

Paphiopedilum
hybrid

PHALAENOPSIS HYBRID

PHALAENOPSIS CHRISTY WHEELER 'JOSHUA' ×
PHALAENOPSIS ANGEL DANCER 'SHOWGIRL' AM/AOS

Genus name is from the Greek phalaina *(moth) and* opsis *(appearance),*
for the white, mothlike delicacy of some species

The seedling pictured represents a quintessential large white phalaenopsis. This one features a lipstick-red lip; both parents (Christy Wheeler 'Joshua' [Necedah × Andrew Hausermann] × Angel Dancer 'Showgirl') are also red-lipped whites.

The large flowers are evenly spaced, and in the right sort of light, they could be mistaken for large moths in flight. It's also worth noting that the splendid inflorescence in the picture is a secondary flowering; after the primary spike bloomed out, it was cut off immediately above the second node from the bottom, which prompted a second spike about a quarter inch below where the cut was made.

A hybrid phalaenopsis of this type often seems almost constantly in bloom. The plants are of easy culture, often likened to that needed by African violets and other popular flowering and foliage houseplants. It is important that these orchids be watered consistently, allowing no extremes of wet or dry, and that they have good air movement about them at all times.

TYPE: Epiphyte

GROWTH HABIT: Monopodial

ORIGINS: Warm Philippine lowlands, India, southeastern Asia, Indonesia, northern Australia

BLOOMING SEASON: Any time of year

LIGHT: Bright diffused, with little or no direct sun; outdoors, shade carefully from direct rays through midday; indoors in or near a bright window, or under fluorescents or high-intensity light

TEMPERATURE: Warm, with winter minimum of 60°–65°F; a noticeable drop from day to night of at least 10°F encourages budding and a longer bloom period

HUMIDITY: Medium to high; inconsistency can cause damage to buds; protect from drafts

MOISTURE: Water consistently all year, especially when in active growth; water plants in place to avoid uneven growth

GROWING MEDIUM: A or B; a combination of medium bark, perlite, and chopped sphagnum moss is common

FERTILIZER: Lightly, regularly, consistently during growth period

PLANT SHOWN: Blooming in spring in a 6-inch pot

Phalaenopsis
hybrid

PHALAENOPSIS HYBRID

PHALAENOPSIS EQUESTRIS × SELF
(SYNS. *STAUROGLOTTIS EQUESTRIS; PHALAENOPSIS
STAUROGLOTTIS; P. ESMERELDA; P. RITEIWANENSIS; P. ROSEA*)

Genus name is from the Greek phalaina *(moth) and* opsis *(appearance),
for the white, mothlike delicacy of some species*

This is hands-down one of the best beginner orchids. The plants commonly spike more than once a year, and it's not unusual for them to be everblooming. They do best in small pots, in a bright spot with little or no direct sun, in normal house or office temperatures. *Phalaenopsis equestris* is an ideal orchid for growing under fluorescent lights and is a good companion for African violets and other gesneriads, and for countless bromeliads. If flowered-out spikes are left in place, they often produce plantlets (keikis) at the tips.

A compact or miniature multiflora, *P. equestris* bears many small, delicate blooms in foot-long branching sprays, a habit that has made it valuable in breeding work. The inflorescence is more or less erect. The flowers are variable as to size (between 1 and 2 inches), color (from pure white to dark rose), and even form (some having liplike petals). The fleshy leaves grow up to 8 inches long and may be plain green or blushed purple on the reverse.

TYPE: Epiphyte

GROWTH HABIT: Monopodial

ORIGINS: Philippines, Taiwan

BLOOMING SEASON: Fall–winter, or at any time of year

LIGHT: Bright diffused, with little or no direct sun. Outdoors, shade carefully from direct rays through midday; indoors in or near a bright window, or under fluorescents or high-intensity light

TEMPERATURE: Warm, with winter minimum of 60°–65°F; a noticeable drop from day to night of at least 10°F encourages budding and a longer bloom period

HUMIDITY: Medium to high; constant; inconsistency can cause buds to blast, wither, and fall before opening; protect from all drafts

MOISTURE: Water consistently all year, especially when in active growth; water plants in place to avoid their reorienting to light after being moved, which can thwart symmetry

GROWING MEDIUM: A or B; a combination of medium bark, perlite, and chopped sphagnum moss is commonly used

FERTILIZER: Lightly, regularly during active growth

PLANT SHOWN: Blooming in summer in a 3-inch pot

Phalaenopsis
hybrid

PHALAENOPSIS HYBRID

PHALAENOPSIS HAUSERMANN'S GALAXY 'STARDOM' × *PHALAENOPSIS* FANCY FREE 'SCARLET SPRING'

Genus name is from the Greek phalaina *(moth) and* opsis *(appearance), for the white, mothlike delicacy of some species*

As the number of gardeners has increased, so too have the ranks of orchid growers. And within this specialization, those who collect and grow phalaenopsis represent a relatively huge populace. Mindful of the possibility that familiarity could inevitably breed a certain contempt, orchid merchants have turned to the "art shades" and other novelties such as spots, stripes, and multiflora habit.

Although the orchid shown is considered a "novelty" phalaenopsis, the color being loosely defined as art shade, it has an impressive family tree. It is from a cross of Hausermann's Galaxy (Prairie du Chien × Cherokee Chief) 'Stardom' × Fancy Free (Aileen Charger × California Love) 'Scarlet Spring'.

A phalaenopsis like the one pictured can be coaxed to bloom twice yearly. The flowers on this type tend to appear in lesser numbers than in the more common varieties, and on shorter, more upright stems. They are, however, long-lasting on the plants, up to two months or more.

TYPE: Epiphyte

GROWTH HABIT: Monopodial

ORIGINS: Parts of Philippines, India, southeastern Asia, Indonesia, northern Australia

BLOOMING SEASON: Any time of year

LIGHT: Bright diffused, with little or no direct sun. Outdoors, shade carefully from direct rays through midday; indoors in or near a bright window, or under fluorescents or high-intensity light

TEMPERATURE: Warm, with winter minimum of 60°–65°F; a noticeable drop from day to night of at least 10°F encourages budding and a longer bloom period

HUMIDITY: Medium to high; constant; inconsistency can cause buds to blast, wither, and fall before opening; protect from all drafts

MOISTURE: Water consistently all year, especially when in active growth; water plants in place to avoid their reorienting to light after being moved, which can thwart symmetry

GROWING MEDIUM: A or B; a combination of medium bark, perlite, and chopped sphagnum moss is commonly used

FERTILIZER: Lightly, regularly during active growth

PLANT SHOWN: Blooming in summer in a 4-inch pot

Phalaenopsis
hybrid

PHALAENOPSIS HYBRID

PHALAENOPSIS HEAVEN'S PRIDE × PHALAENOPSIS GLORIOSO

Genus name is from the Greek phalaina *(moth) and* opsis *(appearance),*
for the white, mothlike delicacy of some species

This is a wonderfully large-flowered white phalaenopsis; words are inadequate to describe its exquisite, ethereal beauty. Phalaenopsis flowers of this type last for up to two months on the plant, and sometimes three. They are also excellent cut for home display, wedding bouquets, wrist corsages, and hair decorations.

The normally winter-flowering white species *Phalaenopsis aphrodite,* which can tolerate 55°F nights, often figures somewhere in the background of large-flowered, modern white moth orchids. Its flowers are smaller and less rounded than those on the plant pictured.

A rule of thumb in staking phalaenopsis is to make a loose tie to a slender cane when the inflorescence is about 4 inches high and again when it reaches about 8 inches. Thereafter, it can be allowed to grow into a natural, graceful arch without further staking or tying.

TYPE: Epiphyte

GROWTH HABIT: Monopodial

ORIGINS: Warm Philippine lowlands; India, southeastern Asia, Indonesia, northern Australia

BLOOMING SEASON: Any time of year

LIGHT: Bright diffused, with little or no direct sun. Outdoors, shade carefully from direct rays through midday; indoors in or near a bright window, or under fluorescents or high-intensity light

TEMPERATURE: Warm, with winter minimum of 60°–65°F; a noticeable drop from day to night of at least 10°F encourages budding and a longer bloom period

HUMIDITY: Medium to high; constant; inconsistency can cause buds to blast, wither, and fall before opening; protect from all drafts

MOISTURE: Water consistently all year, especially when in active growth; water plants in place to avoid their reorienting to light after being moved, which can thwart symmetry

GROWING MEDIUM: A or B; a combination of medium bark, perlite, and chopped sphagnum moss is commonly used

FERTILIZER: Lightly, regularly during active growth

PLANT SHOWN: Blooming in summer in a 6-inch pot

Phalaenopsis
hybrid

PHALAENOPSIS HYBRID

PHALAENOPSIS VIOLACEA 'WIZARD' × *PHALAENOPSIS VIOLACEA* 'FUCHSIA'

Genus name is from the Greek phalaina *(moth) and* opsis *(appearance), for the white, mothlike delicacy of some species*

*P*halaenopsis violacea is a short plant bearing decidedly star-shaped, fleshy flowers with pink coloring that appear one or two at a time or in succession. They normally bloom in late summer and give off a strong, sweet smell. The leaves grow to 9 inches long and are fleshy, leathery, and oblong-elliptical in shape (with the exception of those in the species type collected in Borneo, which may be nearly round in shape).

Several attributes of *P. violacea* and its offspring set them apart. Their compact habit makes them ideal for growing in fluorescent-light gardens. A unique flower shape and generous fragrance also distinguish them from most other moth orchids. And while the flower count may be low at any given time, it's best not to remove a spike when the last bloom fades because more buds will originate from the tip during the next flowering season.

TYPE: Epiphyte

GROWTH HABIT: Monopodial

ORIGINS: Malaya, Borneo, Sumatra

BLOOMING SEASON: Late summer, fall, or at any time of year

LIGHT: Bright diffused, with little or no direct sun. Outdoors, shade carefully from direct rays through midday; indoors in or near a bright window, or under fluorescents or high-intensity light

TEMPERATURE: Warm, with winter minimum of 60°–65°F; a noticeable drop from day to night of at least 10°F encourages budding and a longer bloom period

HUMIDITY: Medium to high; constant; inconsistency can cause buds to blast, wither, and fall before opening; protect from all drafts

MOISTURE: Water consistently all year, especially when in active growth; water plants in place to avoid their reorienting to light after being moved, which can thwart symmetry

GROWING MEDIUM: A or B; a combination of medium bark, perlite, and chopped sphagnum moss is commonly used

FERTILIZER: Lightly, regularly during active growth

PLANT SHOWN: Blooming in summer in a 6-inch pot

Phalaenopsis
hybrid

PHRAGMIPEDIUM BESSEAE

('FOX VALLEY' FCC/AOS ×
'FOX VALLEY FLAME' AM/AOS)

Genus name is from the Greek phragma *(fence, division) and* pedilon *(slipper),*
literally "divided shoe," referring to the triocular ovary and the slipper-shaped lip

The only truly red orchid of the genus *Phragmipedium* known, this is a gorgeous flower with inch-long petals and sepals, and the mouth of the slipper edged in deep yellow. One to four flowers grow on the erect inflorescence. The light green leaves are linear to narrowly elliptical, about 5 to 6 inches long. Since this orchid makes seeds and reproduces readily in cultivation, considerable variation can be observed in its color, form, and flower size.

The name 'Fox Valley' alone is an indication of superiority, a knockout flower, and a wallop to the wallet for such a small plant.

Most often found in Ecuador, the populations of these orchids have decreased drastically in the wake of rampant collection. Since the plants naturally grow on cliff faces at considerable elevations where water constantly flows, they need more water than other phragmipediums, and cooler temperatures when cultivated in the home.

TYPE: Epiphyte, lithophyte

GROWTH HABIT: Sympodial

ORIGINS: South America north to Panama and Guatemala

BLOOMING SEASON: Early spring–late summer

LIGHT: Medium; outdoors, with protection from sun's hot, direct rays through midday; indoors near a bright window, or under fluorescents or high-intensity light

TEMPERATURE: Cool to intermediate, with winter nighttime temperatures of about 48°–55°F

HUMIDITY: Medium to high, with good air movement

MOISTURE: Keep constantly moist but allow rapid drain-off of excess water

GROWING MEDIUM: A; small pots are preferable

FERTILIZER: 20-20-20 at quarter- to half-strength solution, weekly or every other week during active growth

PLANT SHOWN: Blooming in spring in a 4-inch pot

*Phragmipedium
besseae*

PHRAGMIPEDIUM HYBRID

PHRAGMIPEDIUM CALURUM
(*P. LONGIFOLIUM* × *P.* SEDENII)

Genus name is from the Greek phragma *(fence, division) and* pedilon *(slipper),*
literally "divided shoe," referring to the triocular ovary and the slipper-shaped lip

This orchid closely resembles the more common lady's-slipper paphiopedilums. However, it's the habit of phragmipediums such as Calurum to bloom successively, one flower at a time, as the inflorescence continues to elongate. Since the two genera (*Paphiopedilum* and *Phragmipedium*) are now being used together in breeding work, this habit will likely have considerable impact on the entire genre of lady's-slipper orchids.

An outstanding difference between growing this orchid and paphiopedilums is the phragmipediums' appreciation of a marked difference between day and night temperatures. A 25°F temperature drop is ideal, from 75°F in the daytime to about 50°F at night.

Calurum's similarly colored (pale yellow-green, with dark green veins and light purple edging) parent, *P. longifolium,* is a short, several-leaved terrestrial plant with a tendency to grow in large clumps. It is closely related to *P. klotzscheanum,* from which it differs in its shorter, stouter habit. The natural distribution for *P. longifolium* is Costa Rica, Panama, Ecuador, and Colombia. The other parent, *P. sedenii,* has white and rose-pink flowers.

TYPE: Epiphyte, lithophyte, terrestrial

GROWTH HABIT: Sympodial

ORIGINS: South America north to Panama and Guatemala

BLOOMING SEASON: Spring–summer

LIGHT: Medium; outdoors, with protection from sun's hot, direct rays through midday; indoors near a bright window, or under fluorescents or high-intensity light

TEMPERATURE: Intermediate, with a winter minimum of 55°F; avoid temperatures over 90°F

HUMIDITY: High, with good air circulation

MOISTURE: Keep constantly moist but allow rapid drain-off of excess water

GROWING MEDIUM: A; small pots are preferable; divide infrequently to build up a specimen plant with several spikes blooming at once

FERTILIZER: 20-20-20 at quarter- to half-strength solution weekly or every other week during active growth

PLANT SHOWN: Blooming in summer in a 7-inch pot

Phragmipedium
hybrid

POTINARA HYBRID

UNNAMED HYBRID OF ✕ *POTINARA*
(✕ *LAELIOCATTLEYA* ACKER'S MADISON 'KYLE' ✕
✕ *POTINARA* MEMORIA DEANA SANDERS)

A quadrigeneric hybrid first created in 1922 by combining Brassavola, Cattleya, Laelia,
and Sophronitis; *genus named for Monsieur Potin, a French orchid grower*

This gorgeous orchid looks and acts like a *Cattleya*. It is, however, an extraordinary genetic blend combining four distinct but closely related genera: *Brassavola* (source for the oversize, showy lip), *Cattleya* (large flower size), *Laelia* (multiflora trait), and *Sophronitis* (vivid color, rounded flowers). Because of the complex parentage, orchids of ✕ *Potinara* often come into flower three times a year, with blooms that last a month. Add to all of this a light, fresh-air scent, and the result is a near-perfect plant.

The seedling shown is a cross between ✕ *Laeliocattleya* Acker's Madison 'Kyle' (*Cattleya* Portia ✕ Madison Green; a favorite multiflora pink for fall) and ✕ *Potinara* Memoria Deana Sanders, itself a favorite among collectors. Numerous other ✕ *Potinara* hybrids show off the orange-red coloration of the *Sophronitis* genes, as well as the glowing yellow-golds, apricot, and peach.

TYPE: Epiphyte

GROWTH HABIT: Sympodial

ORIGINS: Tropical Central and South America

BLOOMING SEASON: Fall–winter

LIGHT: Medium to high; outdoors, with sufficient filtering of direct rays to avoid sunburn; indoors in a sunny window, or under multiple fluorescents or high-intensity light

TEMPERATURE: Intermediate, with a winter minimum of 55°–60°F

HUMIDITY: Medium to high, with good air circulation

MOISTURE: Water generously in spring and summer, drying a bit between waterings; less in fall and winter, but never allow to become so dry as to shrivel the pseudobulbs

GROWING MEDIUM: A

FERTILIZER: Lightly, frequently during spring and summer, less in fall and winter

PLANT SHOWN: Blooming in fall in a 7-inch pot

Potinara
hybrid

POTINARA HYBRID

×*POTINARA* KATIE STROMSLAND
'GREAT-GRANDCHILD #1'

A quadrigeneric hybrid first created in 1922 by combining Brassavola, Cattleya, Laelia,
and Sophronitis; *genus named for Monsieur Potin, a French orchid grower*

For a relatively compact plant, this complex hybrid is an absolute knockout. Despite it's small overall size, the glorious flowers span 5 to 6 inches across. 'Great-grandchild #1' is the progeny of a cross between Hausermann's Imperial and ×*Sophrolaeliocattleya* Wendy's Valentine, and was registered by Hausermann in 1995.

The small-size plant and big flower show make this orchid ideal for the collector who is looking to maximize a small growing area, such as a home greenhouse, a bay window, or a space illuminated by multiple fluorescents or high-intensity light. In a larger collection, where a sizable greenhouse may be devoted to cattleyas and allied orchids, ×*Potinara* will fit in quite well. The plants are uncomplicated in terms of cultural needs, despite their quadrigeneric status.

TYPE: Epiphyte

GROWTH HABIT: Sympodial

ORIGINS: Tropical Central and South America

BLOOMING SEASON: Fall–winter

LIGHT: Medium to high; outdoors, with sufficient filtering of direct rays to avoid sunburn; indoors in a sunny window, or under multiple fluorescents or high-intensity light

TEMPERATURE: Intermediate, with a winter minimum of 55°–60°F

HUMIDITY: Medium to high, with good air circulation

MOISTURE: Water generously during spring and summer, drying a bit between waterings; less in fall and winter, but never allow to become so dry as to shrivel the pseudobulbs

GROWING MEDIUM: A

FERTILIZER: Lightly, frequently during spring and summer, less in fall and winter

PLANT SHOWN: Blooming in fall in a 5-inch pot

Potinara
hybrid

PSYCHOPSIS HYBRID

PSYCHOPSIS PAPILIO
(*ONCIDIUM PAPILIO* 'PETER' × *ONCIDIUM PAPILIO* 'HAPPY')

Genus name is from the Greek psyche *(butterfly) and* opsis *(resembling),*
evoking the splendid similarity of some species to tropical butterflies

The fabulously constructed and colored flowers of the *psychopsis* orchids were extremely popular during the Victorian period. Single flowers appear successively at the tip of the inflorescence, which grows to about 40 inches tall, and often last for months.

Psychopsis papilio bears orange-brown blossoms marked with yellow and measuring about 4 inches across. The lip carries a large yellow spot on its center. The stiff, dark green leaves, mottled in red or purple, are oblong-elliptical and about 8 inches long and a little over 2 inches wide.

While butterfly orchids of this type have been recognized at least since 1825, it was not until 1975 that they were firmly moved from the *Oncidium* genus to *Psychopsis*. However, in terms of registration and for awarding, the appellation *Oncidium papilio* continues to be used. The seedling shown is larger and showier than the species itself.

TYPE: Epiphyte

GROWTH HABIT: Sympodial

ORIGINS: Trinidad, Venezuela, Colombia, Ecuador, Peru

BLOOMING SEASON: Late spring–early fall

LIGHT: Moderate sun and shade; outdoors, with enough filtering of sun's rays through midday to prevent leaf scorch; indoors in or near a sunny window, or under multiple fluorescents or high-intensity light; avoid northern exposure except while actually in bloom

TEMPERATURE: Intermediate, with a winter minimum of 55°–65°F

HUMIDITY: Moderate, with good air movement

MOISTURE: Water often when growing actively; allow to dry a bit in between

GROWING MEDIUM: A, or on a bark mount; small pots are preferable

FERTILIZER: Weakly (one-fourth to one-half strength) during spring and summer

PLANT SHOWN: Blooming in late spring in a 3-inch pot

Psychopsis hybrid

STELLAMIZUTAARA HYBRID

✕STELLAMIZUTAARA KELLY 'MINI-MAGIC'

Man-made genus combining Brassavola, Broughtonia, *and* Cattleya

'Mini-Magic' seems to have "unique" written all over it. And considering the complexity and richness of its gene bank—*Brassavola nodosa* × ✕*Cattleytonia* Keith Roth (*Cattleya* bicolor × *Broughtonia sanguinea*)—it's no surprise.

The pseudobulbs and leaves, to 12 inches tall, do resemble those of the brassavola parent, and the flowers in art shades are reminiscent of the cattleytonia, 3 to 4 inches across.

This orchid will do best if it can be exposed to fairly high light intensities outdoors in summer, or grown in an air-conditioned greenhouse through the season of longest days. Good air circulation is necessary to prevent leaf scorch, along with adequate moisture at the roots and in the air surrounding the plant to keep the leaves plump.

The indoor gardener who succeeds with *Brassavola nodosa* probably has a good chance of repeating the success with ✕*Stellamizutaara*. Considering the rarity of the plant compared to other orchids, some will find this an irresistible challenge. The usual flowering time of fall and winter is also an advantage for those who yearn for flowers when the garden is frozen over.

TYPE: Epiphyte

GROWTH HABIT: Sympodial

ORIGINS: Central and South America

BLOOMING SEASON: Fall–winter

LIGHT: Medium to high; outdoors, with filtered to direct sun, but protected at midday; indoors in a sunny window, or under multiple fluorescents or high-intensity light

TEMPERATURE: Medium to high, with a winter nighttime low of 55°–65°F

HUMIDITY: High, with good air movement

MOISTURE: Water generously, then pemit to dry slightly before dousing again

GROWING MEDIUM: A

FERTILIZER: Lightly, frequently, regularly, consistently in spring and summer

PLANT SHOWN: Blooming in spring in an 8-inch pot

Stellamizutaara
hybrid

TRUDELIA ALPINA

(SYN. *VANDA ALPINA*)

Genus named for Niklaus Trudel, a Swiss orchid grower and natural history photographer

At first glance, there may be a curious impression of blueness about this orchid's flowers—even though it's not visible under close inspection. The flowers are faintly fragrant and measure 1 to 1½ inches across, with petals and sepals appearing in a range of greens. The fleshy lip is striped in yellow and blackish purple. This orchid's thick, leathery leaves grow horizontally from the stalk and measure 4 to 5 inches long by ½ inch wide.

Trudelia alpina is an uncharacteristically short orchid as compared to the closely allied genus *Vanda,* which is dominated by tall plants. *T. cristata* (syn. *Vanda cristata*), from Nepal and Bhutan, has pale green flowers; its lips are white with purple markings. *T. pumila,* from the northwestern Himalayas and China to Sumatra, has white flowers, a purple striped lip, and a nectar spur uncharacteristic of other species in the genus.

TYPE: Epiphyte

GROWTH HABIT: Monopodial

ORIGIN: Northeastern India

BLOOMING SEASON: Spring–summer

LIGHT: Medium to high; outdoors, with enough diffusion of direct rays through midday to prevent leaf scorch; indoors in the brightest conditions possible without sunburning the leaves, or under multiple fluorescents or high-intensity light

TEMPERATURE: Intermediate, with a winter minimum of 55°F

HUMIDITY: Medium to high, with constant air movement

MOISTURE: Water freely during spring and summer, less in fall and winter, but take care not to let the plant dry to the point of shriveling the leaves

GROWING MEDIUM: A

FERTILIZER: Lightly, frequently, regularly in spring and summer

PLANT SHOWN: Blooming in summer in an 8-inch pot

*Trudelia
alpina*

VANDA HYBRID

VANDA COERULEA 'EDWIN' × SELF

Genus name is from a Sanskrit word for an orchid now known as Vanda tessellata

This vanda hybrid is treasured for its blue flowers, which vary from pale (as in the seedling shown) to strikingly dark. The darker the blue, the more their tesselation (which appears as a checkered effect) stands out. *Vanda coerulea* was crossed with *Euanthe sanderiana* to produce the famous ×*Vandanthe* Rothschildiana, known for its large, flat, incredibly blue flowers.

The individual flowers on this seedling measure 2½ to 3 inches across, nicely spaced out on an inflorescence that grows to 2 feet tall.

Growers have different ideas about the proper way to grow vandas, in particular whether to set them in hanging baskets or to pot them. The former allows the stems to find their own way, creating a phantasmagorical effect—a twisting, turning plant with long-lasting, glorious flowers in season. The latter ties them into a rather rigidly upright stance and yields a formal, symmetrical specimen that is better suited to display in traditional interiors.

TYPE: Epiphyte

GROWTH HABIT: Monopodial

ORIGIN: India, Burma, Thailand

BLOOMING SEASON: Spring–summer

LIGHT: Medium to high; outdoors, with enough diffusion of direct rays through midday to prevent leaf scorch; indoors in the brightest conditions possible without sunburning the leaves, or under multiple fluorescents or high-intensity light

TEMPERATURE: Intermediate to cool, with a winter minimum of 50°F; prefers cooler nights than most vandas, but can be managed in a cattleya house by placement in a cool spot

HUMIDITY: Medium to high, with constant air movement

MOISTURE: Water freely during spring and summer, less in fall and winter, but take care not to let the plant dry to the point of shriveling the leaves

GROWING MEDIUM: A

FERTILIZER: Lightly, frequently, regularly in spring and summer

PLANT SHOWN: Blooming in summer in an 8-inch pot

Vanda
hybrid

VANDA HYBRID

VANDA COERULESCENS 'PETITE ROYALE' × SELF

Genus name is from a Sanskrit word for an orchid now known as Vanda tessellata

This miniature vanda is treasured for its floriferous habit and exceptional pale blue flowers with dark blue-purple lips. While not suited to climates that have a long, hot summer—unless an air-conditioned greenhouse is available—it is probably somewhat more tolerant of warm conditions than the species itself. In bright light, moderate temperatures, and moist air, the blooms will last about a month.

Vanda coerulescens, known as "the other blue vanda" (besides *V. coerulea*), was discovered in April 1837 in North Burma but was not flowered in captivity until 1869.

V. coerulescens inflorescences are often 20 inches long and bear numerous flowers 1 to 1½ inches in diameter. Originating at a higher elevation than some other species, *V. coerulescens* appreciates cooler temperatures, though not below 48°F.

TYPE: Epiphyte

GROWTH HABIT: Monopodial

ORIGINS: India, China, Burma, Thailand

BLOOMING SEASON: Late spring–early summer

LIGHT: Medium to high; outdoors, with enough diffusion of direct rays through midday to prevent leaf scorch; indoors in the brightest conditions possible without sunburning the leaves, or under multiple fluorescents or high-intensity light

TEMPERATURE: Intermediate to cool, with a winter minimum of 50°F; prefers cooler nights than most vandas, but can be managed in a cattleya house by placement in a cool spot

HUMIDITY: Medium to high, with constant air movement

MOISTURE: Water freely during spring and summer, less in fall and winter, but take care not to let the plant dry to the point of shriveling the leaves

GROWING MEDIUM: A

FERTILIZER: Lightly, frequently, regularly in spring and summer

PLANT SHOWN: Blooming in summer in a 7-inch pot

Vanda
hybrid

VANDA HYBRID

VANDA VARAVUTH × *VANDA* MME. RATTANA

Genus name is from a Sanskrit word for an orchid now known as Vanda tessellata

This large, complex hybrid is found naturally in India. The rounded, tesselated blue-purple flowers, measuring about 3 inches across, appear in generous numbers (five or more) on a strong inflorescence that can grow to 15 inches long.

The approximately 35 different *Vanda* species are known for their glorious, clear colors, including rare blues. The flowers are typically long-lived and may even be fragrant. This genus has contributed to more intergeneric crossings than any other, and can claim a place in the genealogies of 75 new genera.

This orchid is one of a wondrous number of large-flowered hybrid vandas that are available in nearly every color permutation imaginable. Generally, they are suited to intermediate to warm conditions, and the flowers last for up to six weeks. The plants with blue flowers usually need cooler temperatures. Whether the plant is permitted to roam through the air from a hanging basket or is staked upright in a pot, it's vital that the air roots be exposed to constant moist, moving fresh air. Irregularity with watering will result in long, leafless stalks crowned by a few of the most recent leaves toward the top.

TYPE: Epiphyte

GROWTH HABIT: Monopodial

ORIGINS: India, China, Burma, Thailand

BLOOMING SEASON: Late spring–early summer

LIGHT: Medium to high; outdoors, with enough diffusion of direct rays through midday to prevent leaf scorch; indoors in the brightest conditions possible without sunburning the leaves, or under multiple fluorescents or high-intensity light

TEMPERATURE: Intermediate, with a winter minimum of 55°F

HUMIDITY: Medium to high, with constant air movement

MOISTURE: Water freely during spring and summer, less in fall and winter, but take care not to let the plant dry to the point of shriveling the leaves

GROWING MEDIUM: A

FERTILIZER: Lightly, frequently, regularly, except during the shortest days of the year (November through January)

PLANT SHOWN: Blooming in summer in a 7-inch pot

Vanda hybrid

YAMADARA HYBRID

×YAMADARA EVERGREEN 'BRITT'

A hybrid genus created by crossing ×Brassolaeliocattleya *and* Epidendrum

Thus stunning green and lipstick pink flowers are capable of standing out in an acre of spectacular greenhouse orchids. In addition, 'Britt' flowers give off an almost confusing scent—vaguely chemical at first, then mellowing to a certain sweetness—although it's not obtrusive.

This is a medium-size, cattleya-type plant with pseudobulbs to 4 inches tall and strong, leathery leaves to 8 inches long. The flowers, each to 3 inches across, are of multiflora habit and keep well either cut or on the plant for up to a month or more.

× *Yamadara* Evergreen 'Britt' can be easily managed in any orchid collection with the usual plants in the Cattleya Alliance: *Brassavola, Broughtonia, Cattleya, Laelia, Sophronitis,* and innumerable man-made genera and hybrids. Even the neophyte will recognize that this orchid belongs with the cattleyas. Conversely, sophisticated growers may be surprised to learn that these gorgeous flowers belong to the man-made genus × *Yamadara,* and that Evergreen 'Britt' is the result of crossing × *Brassolaeliocattleya* Green Giant × *Epidendrum tampense.*

TYPE: Epiphyte, lithophyte

GROWTH HABIT: Sympodial,

ORIGINS: Tropical America

BLOOMING SEASON: Fall–winter

LIGHT: Medium to high; outdoors, with sufficient filtering of direct rays to avoid sunburn; indoors in a sunny window, or under multiple fluorescents or high-intensity light

TEMPERATURE: Intermediate, with a minimum temperature of 55°–60°F in winter

HUMIDITY: Medium to high, with good air circulation

MOISTURE: Water generously during spring and summer, allowing plants to dry a bit between waterings; less in fall and winter, but never to the point of shriveling the pseudobulbs

GROWING MEDIUM: A

FERTILIZER: Lightly, frequently, consistently in spring and summer, less in fall and winter

PLANT SHOWN: Blooming in fall in an 8-inch pot

Yamadara hybrid

ZYGOPETALUM HYBRID

ZYGOPETALUM ARTUR ELLE 'STONEHURST' AM/RHS × *ZYGOPETALUM* ARTUR ELLE 'GEYSERLAND'

Genus name is from the Greek zygon *(yoke) and* petalon *(petal), in reference to the thick callus that seems to yoke together the petals and sepals at the base of the column*

Zygopetalum orchids are famous for their striking flowers, in hues of green, blue, purple, brown, and white, which often last for up to a month. They also give off a haunting fragrance that may evoke memories of walking into a winter garden room redolent with a myriad of spring flowers in bloom—freesias, orange blossoms, narcissus, hyacinths . . .

The outstanding seedling pictured has an inflorescence about 12 inches high, arising from the base of a new growth, and four large flowers, each more than 3 inches across. An older plant can be nearly twice as tall and have upward of a dozen flowers. Mature leaves can grow to nearly 2 feet tall and 2 inches wide, making zygopetalums attractive foliage plants.

TYPE: Epiphyte, terrestrial

GROWTH HABIT: Sympodial, with deciduous pseudobulbs

ORIGINS: South America

BLOOMING SEASON: Fall–spring

LIGHT: Medium; outdoors, with ample shade to prevent leaf scorch; indoors in or near a bright window, or under multiple fluorescents or high-intensity light

TEMPERATURE: Intermediate, with a winter minimum of 55°F

HUMIDITY: Medium to high, with good air circulation

MOISTURE: Water year-round so as to maintain a fairly even condition about the roots; avoid extremes of wet and dry

GROWING MEDIUM: A or B; well drained, in sufficiently large pots to accommodate the large, vigorous roots

FERTILIZER: Lightly, frequently, regularly throughout the growing season; stop for about three months when the new growths have reached full size

PLANT SHOWN: Blooming in fall in a 6-inch pot

Zygopetalum
hybrid

Appendix A

NORTH AMERICAN MAIL-ORDER SOURCES *for* ORCHIDS

The following orchid suppliers issue catalogs and also have places of business open to the public. In recognition and appreciation of Orchids By Hausermann, Inc., where all the orchid portraits were photographed, they are listed first, followed by the other sources in alphabetical order.

ORCHIDS BY HAUSERMANN, INC.
2N134 Addison Rd.
Villa Park, IL 60181-1191
PHONE: 630-543-6855

A&P ORCHIDS
110 Peters Rd.
Swansea, MA 02777
PHONE: 508-675-1717

BLOOMFIELD ORCHIDS
251 W. Bloomfield Rd.
Pittsford, NY 14534
PHONE: 716-381-4206

CARTER AND HOLMES ORCHIDS
629 Mendenhall Rd.
P.O. Box 668
Newberry, SC 29108
PHONE: 803-276-0579

EVERGLADES ORCHIDS, INC.
1101 Tabit Rd.
Belle Glade, FL 33430
PHONE: 561-996-9600

FENDER'S FLORA, INC.
4315 Plymouth Sorrento Rd.
Apopka, FL 32712
PHONE: 407-886-2464

FOX VALLEY ORCHIDS, LTD.
1980 Old Willow Rd.
Northbrook, IL 60062
PHONE: 847-205-9660

GEMSTONE ORCHIDS
5750 E. River Rd.
Minneapolis, MN 55432
PHONE: 612-571-3300

KENSINGTON ORCHIDS
3301 Plyers Mill Rd.
Kensington, MD 20895
PHONE: 301-933-0036

KLEHM GROWERS, INC.
44 W. 637 State Rt. 72
Hampshire, IL 60140-4766
PHONE: 847-683-4761

MIAMI ORCHIDS
22150 S.W. 147 Ave.
Miami, FL 33170
PHONE: 800-516-5348

ORCHIDS LIMITED
4630 N. Fernbrook Lane
Plymouth, MN 55446
PHONE: 612-559-6425

PARKSIDE ORCHID NURSERY, INC.
2503 Mountainview Dr. (Rt. 563)
Ottsville, PA 18942
PHONE: 610-847-8039

R.F. ORCHIDS, INC.
28100 S.W. 182nd Ave.
Homestead, FL 33030
PHONE: 305-245-4570

ROD McLELLAN CO.
914 S. Claremont St.
San Mateo, CA 94402-1834
PHONE: 800-4-ORCHID

SMITH & HAWKEN
Corporate Headquarters
117 E. Strawberry Dr.
Mill Valley, CA 94941
PHONE: 800-776-3336*

STEWART ORCHIDS
P.O. Box 550
Carpinteria, CA 93014
PHONE: 800-621-2450

*Call for general information, to request a catalog, or for retail store addresses, where you can find a large selection of orchid varieties.

Appendix B

GLOSSARY *of* COMMON TERMS

antelope-type: a type of dendrobium in which the two upper petals are decidedly twisted in the manner of an antelope's horns.

bifoliate: plants in the cattleya alliance having two (a pair) of leaves growing from the top of the pseudobulb.

epiphyte: a plant native to a rain forest—or other place where the average humidity is high—that lives off the air, usually on other plants, but is not parasitic.

inflorescence: the flowers and their arrangement on a stalk or stemlike support.

intermediate: hybrids that appear to resemble equal parts of each parent; or, in another context, a range of temperatures, neither chilly nor outright hot, about 55°–85°F.

lithophyte: a plant that naturally makes it home on rocks or in rocky soil, and gains most of its sustenance by absorbing nutrients from the atmosphere.

mericlone: an orchid identical to the plant from which it has been meristemmed, also termed tissue-culturing or cloning.

meristemming: the practice of reproducing orchids (and other plants) by cloning or tissue-culturing, or by multiplying them from a minuscule piece of plant tissue that contains the DNA for the offspring to grow into a mature plant exactly like the one from which it was taken.

pendent: as applied to orchids, it usually refers to an inflorescence that hangs or displays the individual flowers in an arching or nodding position.

pseudobulbs: the swollen, bulblike stems common to many sympodial orchids. The purpose is for storing moisture in order to sustain the orchid plant through normal periods of dry weather.

raceme: an inflorescence, indeterminate, unbranched, and typically elongated, bearing flowers on pedicels at different intervals.

species orchid: a particular orchid plant that occurs in nature and has been declared a true species. It is not a hybrid created in nature without human assistance. Historically, this status has been subject to change, owing to continued research.

spike: a layman's term for the inflorescence of an orchid, in particular with reference to a newly discovered, emerging flowerbud; to say an orchid is "in spike" means that it is about to bloom.

tepals: this term was coined to apply to both the sepals and the petals of an orchid, excepting the lip or labellum.

terete/semiterete: an orchid leaf that is cylindrical or appears circular in cross section.

terrestrial: An orchid that grows in the ground, as opposed to in the air.

type species: an orchid plant whose characteristics are exactly like those ascribed to it by the author of its original, official description.

unifoliate: an orchid plant in the cattleya alliance that produces one leaf from each pseudobulb.

Appendix C

PHOTOGRAPHY CREDITS

PHOTO EDITOR: Alexandra Truitt; PHOTO RESEARCH: Jerry Marshall

Page i Elvin McDonald; *ii* Linda Burgess; *2* Rod Planck; *3* Steven McDonald; *4* Friedriech Strauss; *5* Steven McDonald; *8, 10* Elvin McDonald; *11* Steven McDonald: *12* Viviane Moos; *14* Ray Elliott, Jr.; *15* Lynne Brotchie; *17, 20* Friedrich Strauss; *22* Lanontagne; *25* Photos Horticultural; *26* Jacqui Hurst: *30* Elvin McDonald; *32* all by Steven McDonald; *34* Don Saetzer; *36* Photos Horticultural; *38* Steven McDonald; *39, 40* Photos Horticultural. All photos on *pp. 44-243* by Steven McDonald